Scotland's Winter Mountains with one axe

Scotland's Winter Mountains with one axe

Words and photos Garry Smith

Cover Gav McGrath

Published by Northern Edge Books January 2018

Printed by Gomer Press, in the UK

Distribution Cordee cordee.co.uk

ISBN 978-1-5272-1722-5

reprinted November 2018

revised February 2021

reprinted September 2023

Any activity in the mountains carries with it a danger of personal injury or worse. Participants in these activities should be aware of and accept these risks and be responsible for their own actions. The information in this guide is given in good faith but cannot be taken as fact. It is essential that individuals make judgements for themselves (nobody else can decide whether a burn is too high to cross or if a snow slope is stable enough to climb). The author and publisher can accept no liability for damage to property nor for personal injury or death resulting from the use of this publication.

© Garry Smith 2018 All rights reserved. No part of this publication may be reproduced, stored in or introduced into a retrieval system, or transmitted, in any form or by any means (electronic, mechanical, photocopying, recording or otherwise), without the prior written permission of the author.

Scotland's Winter Mountains with one axe

Preface 'The inexplicable feeling of wellbeing that only occurs during periods of high pressure in Scotland's winter mountains' – I can't for the life of me remember where I read this, but I have no problem recalling that I immediately understood exactly what was being described. Once you get it, well that's it; these mountains have a hold on you for life.

Within this book, a guidebook of sorts, you'll find descriptions of thirty journeys through the Scottish mountains - journeys that can be done with a single axe, in a traditional mountaineering style. All are easily accessible and possible to complete within a winter's day. Each will take you to a beautiful part of the Highlands. And if I've got it right, there should be something for everyone.

Acknowledgements While biffing around in the mountains, gathering route information and photos, I've enjoyed the company of some ace people. Being on the hill with them has been a proper hoot and ensured that whatever happens, doing this book was always worthwhile. I'd especially like to thank Paul James, Kath James, Sheila van Lieshout and Steve Worth, for accompanying me on so many occasions.

Thanks also to the following people for their excellent company; most are long-held friends, a few I met only for the first time, when through whatever circumstance, we ended up sharing time in the mountains – Adam Fisher, Alexis Jones, Andy Ollerton, Andy Camis, Barry Kerslake, Dave Lees, Dave McGimpsey, Dave Smith, Dom Fawcett, Fiona Weatherall, Gareth Jones, Graham Burns, Heather Morning, Ian 'Pimp' Hey, James Fisher, James Whitmore, Karen McIntyre, Kat Powell, Keith Robertson, Martyn Eade, Matt Hawkins, Nick Carver, Robin Thomas, Sarah Crowsely, Scott Brooks, Sophie Holdstock, Steve Cale, Stevie Butterworth, Storm Bates, Stormé England and Toby Keep.

For proof reading and scrutinising I'm massively indebted to Anne Robertson, Erik Brunskill, James Whitmore, Kate Hampson, Mark Lynden, Paul O'Reilly and Tania Scotland. Additional thanks go to Mark Lynden for the stacks of help with all things related to publishing. And thanks also to Gav McGrath for keeping my design ideas in check.

I'm also grateful to Dave McGimpsey, Donald King, Erik Brunskill, Jamie Hageman and Robin Thomas for help with route queries and sharing their knowledge of the winter mountains. For advice on the intro sections, I'd like to thank Keith Ball, Garry Nicholson and again Donald King and Kath James. And for various reasons, I'm appreciative of the time and help given by Donald Morris, Graham McMahon, John Cousins, Mike Lates, Nigel Shepherd, Ric Potter and Will Hardy.

There's a huge thanks to Brian and Sheila Cottam for the annual winter home in the Highlands. And finally, and most importantly, thanks to Tan and Tòmas.

GS
January 2018

Contents

Introduction
- Highlands map 06
- Selection of routes 08
- Route descriptions and maps 09
- Grading system 09
- Transport 10
- Accommodation 10
- The Right to Roam 10
- The mountain environment 11

Mountain Conditions
- What to expect 12
- Terms used to describe conditions 13
- When to go 13
- Weather forecasts 14
- Avalanche forecasts 16
- Avalanche awareness in Scotland 16

Skills and Equipment
- Skills 19
- Equipment 20
- Mountain rescue 22
- What to do in an emergency 22

Notes
- Mountain names 152

Crossing the Allt Coire Ardair, heading for Raeburn's Gully on Creag Meagaidh - Sheila van Lieshout

Contents

East Highlands
01	Lochnagar	The Black Spout	I	24
02	Northern Cairngorms	Over the Back	I	27
03	Northern Cairngorms	The Fiachaill Ridge	I/II	34

Northwest Highlands
04	An Teallach	The Ridge Traverse	II	38
05	An Teallach	Hayfork Gully	I/II	43
06	Beinn Eighe	The Black Carls	I	47
07	Beinn Eighe	Morrison's Gully	I	50
08	Liathach	Main Ridge Traverse	II	54
09	Liathach	North-South Crossing	I	58
10	Beinn Alligin	Deep South Gully	I	62
11	Beinn Damh	The Traverse	I	66
12	Beinn Bhàn	A' Chioch Traverse	II	69
13	Sgorr Ruadh	Academy Ridge & Post Box Gully	II	73
14	Fuar Tholl	The Crossing	I	77

Skye
15	Sgùrr nan Gillean	The Traverse	II	80
16	Bruach na Frithe	via Sgùrr a' Bhàsteir	I/II	86

Northwest Highlands
17	The Saddle	Forcan Ridge	I/II	91
18	Aonach air Chrith	North Ridge	I	96

Central Highlands
19	Beinn a' Chaorainn	East Ridge	I	99
20	Creag Meagaidh	Raeburn's Gully	I	102

West Highlands
21	Càrn Dearg Meadhonach	East Ridge	I	107
22	Ben Nevis	Càrn Mòr Dearg Arête	I	112
23	Ben Nevis	Ledge Route	II	116
24	Ben Nevis	South Castle Gully	I/II	121
25	Stob Bàn	South Gully	I	125
26	Beinn a' Bheithir	The Two Ridges	I	129
27	Aonach Eagach	The Traverse	II	134
28	Stob Coire nam Beith	Summit Gully	I/II	139
29	Stob Coire Sgreamhach	Sròn na Làirig	II	144
30	Buachaille Etive Mòr	Chasm to Crowberry	II	148

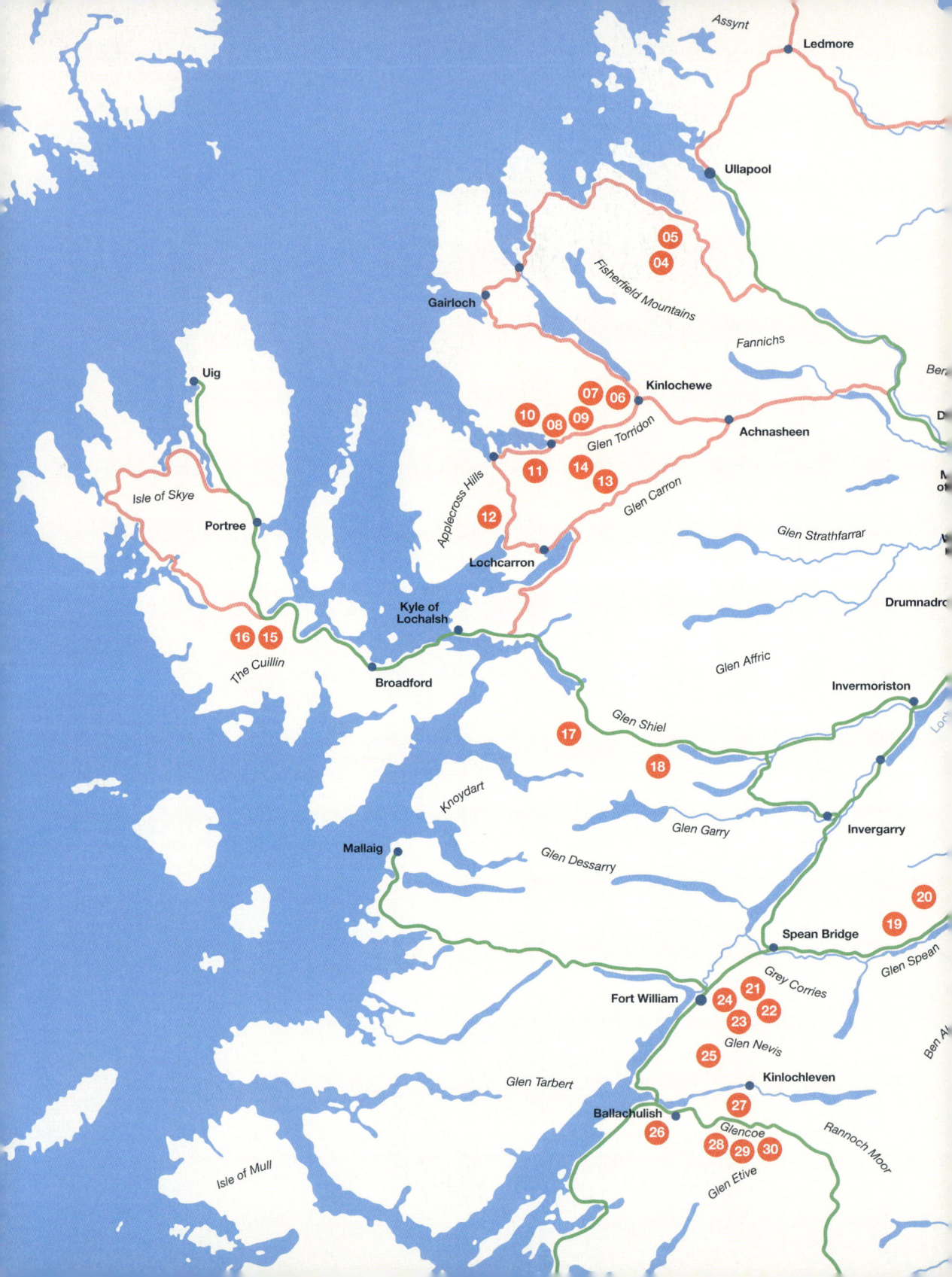

Introduction

The classic view looking east along Liathach's main ridge - Steve Cale, Andy Ollerton and Alexis Jones

The selection Every route in this book is an outstanding winter journey. This was the main criterion for their selection, along with the obvious requirement that they can be done with one axe. Doing any of the routes can be considered as winter mountaineering, since each involves an element of exciting terrain... some a lot more than others. They all suit a lightweight, traditional approach, where only a minimal amount of climbing gear is carried, often no more than a short rope and a few slings.

The selection of routes is personal. It is not a 'best of' by any means, although all the classic easy ridges have been included, along with the big gullies of the Northwest. There is a broad range of technical difficulty within the list and a few routes have been included that provide a nice step-up from winter walking. Regardless of grade, any of the itineraries have the potential to be challenging if the weather doesn't play ball. There has been no attempt to get an even geographical spread across the Highlands; the mountains are where they are. The order in which the routes appear in the guide is purely down to their location and does not reflect their difficulty.

Introduction

Every route on the list can be done in a day; often much quicker if conditions are right and you are going well. Admittedly, a traverse of An Teallach may be a very long day but it's still a day. Some of the routes start with big walk-ins, such as the track to reach Lochnagar or the Coire Lair path leading to Sgorr Ruadh, but these are the exceptions. Most of the mountains in these itineraries are relatively close to a road, and even those that are not can still be classed as easily accessible as far as winter mountaineering goes.

Nothing has been included that isn't regularly 'in nick'. It would take an extraordinarily mild winter for any route not to be in a proper snowy condition and doable at some point in a winter season. No such winter has occurred for two decades prior to publication, but hey, a couple have come very close. Only the two routes on Skye need careful stalking to get done; the Cuillin's proximity to the sea means generally less snow, and when good conditions do arrive they rarely last long. For every other route, the odds are they'll be doable on lots of occasions throughout the season. Not all of the time, but enough of the time to keep your hopes alive.

Route descriptions and maps The descriptions are written so that they can be easily followed using an Ordnance Survey (OS) 1:50,000 map; the most commonly used scale for winter mountaineering. The Harvey's 1:40,000 Mountain Maps, available for Ben Nevis, the Cairngorms and Torridon, are a good alternative and offer more detail without becoming confusing. Grid references are only supplied for the start of routes and for crucial points along the way, such as gully entrances or to give the exact location of the start of a descent from a plateau. Giving more grid references would have made it too easy to load a route directly onto a GPS without first tracing it on a map, an important planning step to go through.

At the start of each description, stats for the distance and total ascent are given for the whole route. Where there is more than one way back to the valley, the stats will refer to the option given precedence in the description. Compass points are abbreviated to capitals when you are meant to head in that direction (N, NNE, NE, etc) and are approximate. The terms left and right refer to when you are facing a cliff. For other situations, the sensible Kiwi mountaineering terms of true left and true right are frequently used to avoid confusion – the true right bank of a stream is the right bank when looking downstream.

The maps in this book are to scale and are very accurate, but are only intended to help planning and for armchair use. Contour lines are drawn at 100m intervals and the resulting bands are coloured according to a standard scale that is the same on every map. A dashed red line corresponds to the described route. A darker dashed line represents an established path or track. Where space allows, any important features mentioned in the text have been named, such as corries, streams and subsidiary peaks.

Grading system The conventional Scottish winter grades used in this book have a currency that is universally understood. Despite each grade's definition giving some technical detail (i.e. slope angle), they are best thought of as simply an indication of the overall difficulty of a route, and have been applied as such. Okay this is very subjective, especially in the vagaries of a Scottish winter, but the system seems to work well. People quickly get in tune and soon know what to expect with 'grade I terrain' or even the nuanced 'steep grade I terrain'.

Grade I	Straightforward snow slopes up to 50 degrees, or simple scrambles on snowed-up or icy rock.
Grade I/II	The difficulty of the route varies dramatically with conditions. Either the higher or lower grade may apply according to the build-up of snow or the presence of ice.
Grade II	Snow slopes up to 60 degrees with the possibility of some steeper but short steps. Tricky scrambling on mixed terrain.

Any gully, regardless of the grade, can at times have a large cornice at its exit - so large that it may be extremely difficult to get past. And even the easiest grade I slope can be a serious climb when severe terrain lies beneath it.

Introduction

Transport There is no shying away from the fact that the only realistic way to get around the Highlands in winter, with the aim of heading into the mountains, is by car. Public transport is sadly too infrequent to even be a consideration. The remote location of starting points, the need to set off early and not knowing when you'll be back down to the valley are just the start of a long list of reasons why using buses would be wholly impractical.

There are perhaps two exceptions when a car is not altogether a necessity. The Cairngorm ski area car park, the starting point for the routes in the Northern Cairngorms, is connected to Aviemore by a regular shuttle bus. It is also very easy to hitch in both directions on the ski area access road, with plenty of skiers and hill-goers willing to offer a lift, even when returning in the dark. The North Face car park in Torlundy, the starting point for routes on Ben Nevis and the Càrn Mòr Dearg Arété, is only 4km from Fort William and it is easy to arrange a drop-off and pick-up by local taxi.

Accommodation The Highlands is really switched on to tourism and every type of accommodation is on offer; hotels, B&Bs, hostels, self-catering chalets and even heated yurts are available throughout the winter months. In less than a decade the internet has revolutionised how accommodation is booked and has in some ways levelled the playing field for smaller and more quirky accommodation providers, making it easier for people to find them. Every aspect of an establishment's facilities will have been reviewed, rated or blogged about, making it an easy exercise to find somewhere suitable to stay. It seems redundant for a guidebook to give anything other than an overview on the subject.

There is no single base that would be convenient for all the routes in this book. Aviemore and Fort William are well placed for the East Highland and West Highland mountains respectively and have an enduring popularity with winter climbers and hill-walkers. Both towns have a broad range of accommodation and all the amenities you could need, including outdoor shops. Car hire can easily be arranged in either town, making them good gateways into the Highlands in general; Aviemore is on the main east coast rail line and Fort William is the final stop on the main west coast line.

Despite the convenience of having every amenity at hand, staying in a town is unlikely to be everyone's idea of a holiday in the Scottish mountains. A scenic Highland village, one with a pub or hotel bar serving hot meals, is perhaps more in keeping with most people's ideal accommodation base. On the east, most of the Spey Valley villages would fit this bill. On the west, Inchree, Onich, Ballachulish and Glencoe all make good bases. In the northwest, Kinlochewe and Lochcarron are just two of a number of villages that are handy for the Torridonian and Coulin Forest mountains. Ullapool is a lovely place to stay if An Teallach is the objective. Broadford is ideally positioned as an overnight stop prior to a day on Skye's Cuillin mountains.

Camping whilst winter mountaineering in Scotland is hardcore and not many people try it more than once. Only a few official campsites remain open during the winter; the most handy being at Glenmore near Aviemore and in Glencoe. Otherwise it is wild camping. Staying in a camper van can work well on short trips so long as there is some facility to properly dry clothing and boots. This is probably needless to say, as people with vans tend to be resourceful and all Highland pubs have fires. Longer trips can always be interspersed with a night under a hostel or hotel roof. Good places to pull over and sleep are everywhere.

It's worth noting that the availability of accommodation is at a premium over the Christmas and Hogmanay period, when securing somewhere to stay may need to be done months in advance. Another busy period will be during the schools' half term week, which is usually but not always the third week of February. It is never as busy as Hogmanay but budget accommodation does tend to fill up quickly, particularly if there are good mountain conditions.

The Right to Roam The Scottish Outdoor Access Code is probably one of the most progressive in the world. The code was written into law in 2005, as part of the Land Reform Act, and gives the statutory right of responsible access onto private land for recreational and educational purposes. The Right to Roam, as the code is informally called, has its roots in the long-standing Scottish belief that there really is no such thing as trespass; that people have freedom of access to Scotland's hills, mountains and wild land. This of course is how it should be but it was never enshrined in law until the passing of the Land Reform Act.

With rights come responsibilities – aim to keep the mountain environment as you find it by keeping your impact to a minimum. Respect the fact that others work on the land and depend on it for their livelihood. Also give every respect to those who enjoy the outdoors in other ways, even if you find their pastimes distasteful. Have some consideration when you're near to residential property and allow privacy. In a nutshell, just don't do the sort of stuff that would nark anyone.

The mountain environment For most hill-goers the Highland's flora and wildlife are an inextricable part of any mountain journey. In fact, it is hard to think of any mountaineer who wouldn't take delight in a chance encounter with a mountain hare on a still winter's day. There are numerous books covering the natural history of Scotland, but only one is dedicated to the Scottish Hills; *Hostile Habitats – Scotland's Mountain Environment*, edited by Nick Kempe and Mark Wrightman, is a highly recommended read. The book offers a detailed yet easily understandable introduction to the natural and man-made environment of Scotland's mountains.

Let's move straight to the main concern, right now there are two major threats to the Highland mountain environment. The first comes from climate change… but not as might initially be thought. Well-intentioned but ill thought-through subsidies have resulted in a Klondike-type rush to construct dams and wind turbines across the Scottish mountains, some being proposed in the most insensitive places imaginable.

The second major threat stems from Scotland's unfair distribution of land ownership (at the time of writing, half the private land in Scotland is owned by just 432 people). Many big landowners still appear to wield the same influence and power as they always have, with some large Highland estates seemingly able to behave with impunity in their unbridled pursuit of revenues; a bulldozed track across every hillside is scarily approaching the norm in some southeast Highland glens.

There is an undeniable need for renewable energy. And there is an absolute necessity to help rural communities earn a sustainable living from the land. But there is also a responsibility to conserve at least some wild land for future generations. For anyone who loves the Scottish mountains, it is incredibly sad that the current planning legislation, intended to balance these needs, appears more of a grand exercise in appeasement rather than any kind of long-term strategy.

Thankfully, there are many individuals and pioneering organisations fighting to safeguard Scotland's mountain environment and also working to create a wilder Scotland to benefit both people and wildlife – The John Muir Trust, Trees for Life, Cairngorms Connect and Coigach & Assynt Living Landscape are just a handful of examples. Most of us will be outraged when we see the unnecessary destruction of wild land, but we'll do little other than blow hot air for a while and sign an online petition. Consider a more active response; think also about supporting organisations like these and join the wider debate.

The mountains and the sea. Climbing up to Sgùrr Beag at the end of Sgùrr nan Gillean's long southeast ridge - Robin Thomas

Mountain Conditions

Returning from Aonach Beag. Large cornices following 4 days of constant westerlies - James Whitmore and Dom Fawcett

What to expect If there is one defining feature of the winter mountain weather in Scotland, it is the huge variability that can occur. These are mountains in which conditions move from one extreme to another at an alarming pace; at times with a degree of unpredictability that can catch out even the savviest of mountaineers. Expect a cold and raw environment. An environment that is beautiful yet hostile, where winds can be so ferocious as to make walking and navigation nigh on impossible. There is very good weather too... and everything else in-between.

Completely fine, blue-sky days in winter are not rare, but they are in the minority. More often than not, a winter's day will be a mixed bag, which at some point will include a period of difficult weather, usually wind. So to get stuff done, it helps to adopt the mind-set that being in the mountains in challenging conditions is the norm in Scotland; 'going for a look', even when there's a poor forecast, is how things get achieved. Obviously common sense needs to prevail; a deteriorating forecast requires respect and days with constant storm force winds, or driving rain at all levels are, like anywhere else in the world, best spent in the valley.

Mountain Conditions

Terms used to describe conditions Throughout this book mountain conditions are mostly referred to using simplistic, non-meteorological terms. They are the same as would be used by the vast majority of winter hill-walkers and climbers when describing conditions encountered on a day out to a mate. Common parlance if you like. Most of these terms are self-explanatory but some need a little clarification. For example, 'good snow conditions' means exactly that, a reasonable cover that supports your weight and is safe. 'Lean conditions', although quite subjective, is simply taken as meaning a less than ideal amount of snow. 'Poor snow conditions' is a slightly ambiguous term but is generally used, in a rather understated way, when there's an avalanche risk.

There are also two technical terms that are widely used when talking about mountain conditions. The thin coating of clear ice on rock, the sort that is desperately slippery to climb over, is always referred to by its universal name, 'verglas'. The term 'névé', although strictly speaking a specific type of re-frozen granular snow, has been commandeered in Scotland as the generic name for any type of hard snow. 'Bomber névé' is used to describe the perfect consistency, that which easily takes the penetration of an axe and is a joy to climb. 'Bullet-hard névé' is as it sounds and is so hard that it is difficult to kick-in with a crampon point. And then there's 'squeaky névé', which, well, squeaks when you walk on it.

The term 'alpine conditions' may also need some explanation. It is used when conditions in the Scottish mountains are thought to be more akin to those found in the bigger continental ranges; usually when there's crystal clear visibility and a dryness to the air. Days like these happen sporadically throughout the season and can arise from the briefest incursion of high pressure. When a major continental high moves in over Scotland it can produce truly sublime alpine conditions, with temperature inversions resulting in balmy conditions on the tops. Despite these high summit temperatures, snow on shaded slopes and in sheltered gullies remains frozen (due to the process of sublimation, which we won't go into), producing, over time, the most beautiful névé on which to climb. Halcyon days.

When to go In this book, it's considered to be winter in the Scottish mountains between the beginning of December and the end of March; and only when there is enough snow-cover to warrant an axe to complete a chosen journey. Okay this is a bit of a woolly definition, but it won't be far off the criteria set by most hill-goers as to what constitutes proper winter in the mountains. And yes, really cold temperatures and major snowstorms often occur outside these months, transforming the mountains into a magical frozen world… but it just isn't winter; the different light and the overall ambiance will always suggest late autumn or early spring.

From a meteorological perspective there is no distinct pattern to Scotland's mountain weather across the winter season. Scotland sits at the crossroads of all sorts of global weather systems, each jostling as to which one has the biggest influence over the Highlands. The greatest arbiter of the type of winter Scotland will experience, the likelihood of a snowy season or not, is the North Atlantic jet stream. A strong jet stream will bring stormy and warmer air directly onto Scotland, whereas a weaker, wavier jet stream may result in much colder conditions. To complicate matters further, the strength of the jet stream can vary dramatically. In essence, there are so many variables affecting Scotland's winter weather that no two winters are ever the same.

In general, certain weather and conditions do tend to occur more frequently at particular times throughout the winter. But, just to re-emphasise, this is not sufficiently consistent to be considered as a pattern, far from it. Bearing this in mind, when is it most likely to snow in the mountains? The early season (throughout December and into January) tends to consist of cold snaps, when substantial snowfalls do occur but are rarely sustained throughout the period. Persistent snowfall, during which a good base to the lying snow starts to build, tends to happen more throughout the core winter period of mid-January through to early March. Beyond early March it regularly continues to snow, sometimes heavily, but usually not with the frequency to continue building to any already established base.

Mountain Conditions

To be honest, trying to figure out the snowiest parts of the winter and thus the best time for a Scottish mountaineering trip is a futile exercise. Sticking to the core winter period of mid-January to early March may be the only reasonable bet, but otherwise it is a lottery as to when the mountains will have a satisfactory snow cover. Those lucky enough to live in Scotland, and able to drop what they're doing, are obviously best placed to take advantage of the coming and going of good weather and wintry conditions throughout the season. For just about everyone else, who will likely need to arrange their holidays in advance, it's just case of rolling with whatever conditions they happen to find.

Scottish winter mountaineering doesn't always mean that you have to resign to taking poor weather on the chin, quite the contrary. Weather and conditions are localised and vary greatly from area to area, hence the regionalised mountain weather and avalanche forecasts. The reliability of the short-range predictions within of these forecasts, coupled with the wealth of up-to-date information available on the internet, means that if you can be flexible about where to go, the chances of a fine day on the hill can be pushed up massively. This means not sticking doggedly to only venturing into the mountains near to your accommodation. Have the discipline to get up early and a willingness to drive, often not that far, to where conditions could be so much better. The rewards can far outweigh the effort.

Weather forecasts Having a good forecast is essential. Without one, any form of planning or the ability to make a sensible route choice goes out the window. The following are the usual ports of call for determining the weather situation in the Scottish mountains. The most popular sources for short-range forecasts are the Mountain Weather Information Service (MWIS) and the Met Office. Both these specialist services give a reasonably accurate picture of what is likely to happen over the following 48 hours. Although both use similar forecasting methods, MWIS generally comes out top when it comes to a crude consensus as to which service is the more trusted. The MWIS format, which outlines what conditions to expect at 900m (roughly Munro level), is certainly the more user-friendly of the two.

Both services also extend their forecasts; MWIS offers a general planning outlook for a week to 10 days ahead whereas the Met Office gives a synopsis for 5 days ahead. Significantly less reliable than the short-range (48 hour) forecasts, these medium-range forecasts can still give a fair indication of whether stable or unsettled weather is on the horizon and the likely wind direction and its anticipated speed. Unless there is a super-stable high-pressure system sitting firmly over Scotland, the accuracy of these forecasts drops off markedly beyond the 3-day forecasting period. MWIS are always upfront when there is low confidence in what they are predicting in the medium-range… a real indication that all bets are off.

A handy feature of the Met Office website is the ability to get a forecast for a number of specific mountain summits. Although impressively detailed, the 3-hourly predictions for summit temperatures within these forecasts are far from accurate but do give an indication of the direction the freezing level is heading throughout the day. Anecdotally, the anticipated summit wind directions and the probability given for good visibility seem more robust, but should still only be taken as indicators.

Another useful feature from the Met Office is the ability to access actual observed weather data, found in the 'Last 24 Hours' section on their website. It is a reliable way of finding out where it has snowed in the Highlands in the preceding day, and for roughly how long. For those who prefer their weather data in a more traditional and raw format, the Met Office site also provides detailed surface pressure charts that are updated every 12 hours.

Both specialist mountain forecasts are issued the afternoon prior to the forecasted period. Most of the time this isn't a concern, but when there is large degree of uncertainty with what's going on with the weather, a more recent forecast can be useful. When the weather pattern is particularly active MWIS will update their forecast early the following morning, or in very volatile situations later the same evening. The Met Office tend to update their forecast in the very early hours of the morning, often as early as 2am. All forecasts clearly show an issue time.

Mountain Conditions

The only TV/media forecasts worth their salt are the general BBC and CH4 weather reports, which are easily accessed via their respective websites. They may not provide specifics such as the anticipated freezing level and summit wind speed for the East Highland mountains but just about all other essential information is in there. Do not assume that the forecasts broadcast in the evenings are the most up to date available, as they will have likely been compiled using data from earlier in the day.

Real time weather information, from the summit weather stations on Aonach Mòr (1130m) and Cairn Gorm (1245m), is freely available online. On the hour temperature readings, plus information on wind speed and direction, provide an accurate gauge of what's currently happening across the tops in both the East and West Highlands. This may be information overload for a lot of people but it has its uses, particularly during a volatile weather period; an unforeseen change in wind direction or a spike in temperature will have an immediate consequence on where any avalanche risk was thought to be.

The Wetterzentrale website is a resource that can both raise hopes and deflate them. It is a central hub from which to access the long-range forecasts put out by the major meteorological organisations around the world. Particularly addictive are the European air-stream and temperature charts, which show the likelihood, or not, of cold air enveloping Scotland in the upcoming 10 days.

Although undoubtedly useful, with the quality of modern forecasts there is no longer a necessity to have an understanding of the underlying meteorological systems that produce Scotland's winter weather. It is enough to appreciate that day-to-day mountain conditions are mainly determined by the direction of the airstream flowing overhead and where that airstream has come from.

In a nutshell, north to northeasterly winds, having originated in the arctic, will be bitterly cold and often produce heavy snowfalls. Conversely, having travelled over the mid-Atlantic, southwesterlies will be warm and wet, resulting in periods of thaw. Easterly winds from Scandinavia and Northern Europe bring very cold and stable weather. Westerlies on the other hand, coming from the north Atlantic, bring cool but fluctuating temperatures and unsettled weather. When there is clash of these air masses, the subtle boundary between warm and cold air can produce a classic mix of rain and snow as freezing levels fluctuate… Scottish conditions!

MWIS	mwis.org.uk
Met Office	metoffice.gov.uk
Wetterzentrale	wetterzentrale.de
Cairn Gorm and Aonach Mòr summit data	weatheronline.co.uk

A spindrift blizzard raging across the northern flanks of Cairn Gorm, seen from the snowgates at Glenmore

Mountain Conditions

Avalanche Forecasts The Scottish Avalanche Information Service (SAIS) is a publicly funded organisation that provides daily snow and avalanche reports for six popular mountain areas – Northern Cairngorms, Southern Cairngorms, Creag Meagaidh, Lochaber, Glencoe and Torridon. The reports are issued online, normally by 5pm, and give an avalanche-hazard forecast for the following day. The level of avalanche risk is rated using a scale of 5 categories ranging from 'Low' to 'Very High', which correspond to those in a standardised and internationally used system. An easy to interpret diagram, in the form of a compass rose, indicates the anticipated level of risk across all slope directions (N, NE, E, etc). The graphics also indicate changes in risk with altitude and whether the hazard is widespread or localised across a particular aspect.

Scottish Avalanche Information Service

sais.gov.uk

Hazard level	Avalanche probability
5 Very High	Widespread natural and human triggered avalanches will occur.
4 High	Natural and human triggered avalanches will occur.
3 Considerable	Natural avalanches possible. Human triggered avalanches are likely.
2 Moderate	Natural avalanches unlikely. Human triggered avalanches possible.
1 Low	Natural avalanches very unlikely. Human triggered avalanches unlikely.

The devil is in the detail with the SAIS reports and only by reading the text can you discover the exact nature of any hazard and where it is thought to lie. There is a comprehensive guide to interpreting the reports on the SAIS website. Forecasters also post photographs onto a daily mountain information blog. These blogs are an educational goldmine, not only do they show how the mountains are looking but often go some way to explaining everyday observations on the hill. They are well worth visiting, whether you have a trip to the Highlands on the horizon or not.

Avalanche awareness in Scotland There is an avalanche risk, to some degree, on most days throughout the winter season. But at the same time, actual avalanches are rare occurrences in the Scottish mountains. Certain notorious but well-documented slopes and gullies will be the scenes of large spontaneous avalanches seemingly every time there is a reasonable snowfall, but these are not representative of the Highlands environment as a whole. The frequency with which avalanches occur is a side issue, the important thing is to acknowledge that they are a very real and pernicious threat. Accidents involving avalanches happen each year, and unfortunately often result in fatalities.

The make-up of the avalanche hazard in the Scottish mountains is somewhat different to that found in the alpine ranges, in that the vast majority of the risk in Scotland is associated with windslab; areas of windblown snow that have built up over the existing snowpack. The hazard in Scotland also has a tendency to manifest itself in relatively small patches of snow, sometimes only a few centimetres thick. Owing to the typical Scottish mountain terrain, anyone triggering these small avalanches is likely to be carried over treacherous or even deadly ground. Most avalanche incidents in Scotland are of this nature; when any injury or fatality is more commonly caused by trauma rather than as a result of being buried.

When it comes to getting a heads up that an avalanche risk exists, and a prediction of where that risk might be, the daily SAIS report is an excellent resource; it is compiled by forecasters with significant expertise and experience of Scottish snow conditions. However, it is important to remember that the report is only a forecast and its predictions are not a certainty; its accuracy is susceptible to any unexpected changes in the weather, no matter how subtle.

Choosing a safe route cannot rely on the avalanche forecast alone. As already said, the hazard can change with just the slightest shift in wind direction or speed, or even with a marginal increase in temperature. Furthermore, the vast majority of the Highlands are not covered by the forecast service. To be properly on it, you'll need to develop your own understanding of the avalanche hazard in Scotland. It isn't rocket science, quite the opposite. A basic grasp of how typical Scottish wind-blown avalanche conditions come about, together with some ability to recognise those conditions when on the hill, are all that's needed to start making safer route choices.

This is not an instructional book, but it would be disingenuous, at the very least, not to give some advice on something as serious as avalanches - especially as a lot of the book's itineraries involve crossing primo avalanche terrain. The following blocks of information offer a very simplistic overview of the 'need to know' stuff. For want of a better term, consider them a lesson plan.

— The likelihood of avalanches will be at its highest during heavy snowfall or drifting and in the 24 hr period afterwards. Unstable conditions will develop when snow is being put down at more than 3cm per hour. Consider a continuous build-up of more than 30cm to be particularly hazardous. The old rule of thumb of 'after a snowstorm wait 48hrs' is pretty sound advice. There will nearly always be a safer alternative to the day you had originally planned. Think ridges.

— The vast majority of avalanche hazard in Scotland is created by snow that has been blown around the mountains and then deposited on leeward or sheltered slopes. This wind-blown snow, made up of crystals damaged by turbulence, forms a layer on top of the existing snowpack and is known as windslab. As the bond between windslab and the snowpack tends to be weak, it creates a risk of the windslab detaching and sliding downhill should you try to cross it. Very strong winds can produce 'hardslab', which may feel solid to walk on but is equally prone to sliding.

— The location of any windslab hazard is dependent upon wind direction; if there is a westerly wind, then wind-blown snow will be deposited as windslab on easterly aspects, and vice versa. Localised wind effects, such as eddies within corries, can create pockets of windslab in random places, where wind-blown snow is deposited in hollows or trapped behind terrain features. Snow blowing across a slope can also accumulate on the sides of gullies or on the flanks of ribs, a process referred to as 'cross loading'.

— There is no reliable method of determining whether a windslab-laden slope is safe to cross. The old-style approach to evaluating snow stability that involved digging an elaborate 'test pit' at the foot of a slope or before a descent, from which a decision to go or not could be made, has been proved to be very unreliable. Sending the big lad across first does not work either. Bear in mind that it is rarely essential to cross a potentially avalanche-prone slope.

— Compared to windslab, other types of avalanche hazard are far less prevalent but are also much harder to identify. A prolonged cold period will likely see the phenomenon of hoar crystals growing on the surface of the snowpack. Any subsequent snowfall will bury these delicate crystals producing a weak layer within the new snowpack. This buried instability will remain in place until the next thaw and on rare occasions can persist as a hazard for weeks. Thankfully, the SAIS reports are very reliable when it comes to flagging up the existence of such layers, which would otherwise remain undetected by the majority of hill-goers. In these instances, it is sensible to extrapolate the SAIS warnings to apply Highland wide, as all of the Scottish mountains will likely be experiencing the same cold conditions.

— A sudden temperature rise can cause specific hazards, with one of the main dangers being the increased risk of cornices collapsing. Warm temperatures, or rain, can produce instabilities on any laden slope, regardless of aspect; the snow will become heavier causing a risk of the actual snowpack fracturing, resulting in a wet snow avalanche. Be conscious that the first hour of rainfall is the most likely time period for this to occur.

Mountain Conditions

— The terrain plays a significant part in the location of avalanche hazards. Almost all windslab avalanches happen on slopes between 25 to 45 degrees, the optimum angle being around 35 degrees (it's a handy skill to be able to recognise when the gradient of a slope is within these angles). Convex (bulging) slopes are particularly dangerous, as any windslab will be under tension. Features such as ravines and narrow valleys, or even flat ground directly beneath slopes, are potential terrain traps; avalanches will have nowhere to disperse and even a small amount of snow could result in burial.

There is obviously far more to understanding the avalanche hazard in Scotland than has been outlined above. However, getting your head around this basic information will help start making sense of what you see as you go along; there are lots of giveaway signs when snow is being moved around and numerous clues to where it is being deposited. There is a tell-tale chalky appearance and distinctive under-foot feel to windslab that quickly becomes easy to recognise. Potential terrain traps in the landscape begin to stand out and any signs of weakness in the snowpack, such as surface cracking, become all too obvious.

To sum up - an avalanche report, a weather forecast and just a basic knowledge of avalanche hazards can give you a very good idea of where any risk is likely to be before you even set foot on the hill. Good route finding in avalanche terrain, based on your observations, is a real skill in which it takes time to become confident. The more mountaineering experience you have, and the more you understand about how snow behaves, the more tactics and options are available to you. Just remember, if there is poor visibility in the mountains, the odds will not be stacked in your favour when making any tricky decisions about route choice.

There are a number of initiatives available to help with safe travel in avalanche terrain. The SAIS 'Be Avalanche Aware' (BAA) is the only one geared specifically towards the Scottish mountains. The decision-making process it outlines, along with its easy-to-digest resources, provides a good, practical and very structured approach to dealing with avalanche hazard. Details of the initiative can be found on the SAIS website, along with a link to a BAA app that can deliver the daily avalanche reports, mountain info blogs and notifications directly to your phone.

Avalanche equipment – A transceiver, shovel and probe (TSP) are not considered as necessary equipment for Scottish winter walking, mountaineering or climbing. The nature of the Scottish avalanche hazard is best dealt with by avoidance tactics and good decision-making. Carrying a TSP does not help with this, and there is no obligation, moral or otherwise, to own them. Your safety on a day's winter mountaineering would be better improved by purchasing a good set of winter tyres.

There are of course exceptions when it would make every sense to carry a TSP. Ski tourers, who at times are moving very quickly through the landscape, cannot always maintain a sense of what is happening with the structure of the surrounding snow. Then there are those who have little choice in being exposed to avalanche risk, such as a mountain rescue team conducting a night-time search in stormy conditions.

Skills and Equipment

Flying back down to Glen Shiel after a quick ascent of Aonach air Chrith's wee north ridge - Sheila van Lieshout

Skills An experienced winter hillwalker is likely to have all the basic skills required for the easier graded routes in this book; competence in using crampons, knowing how to brake with an axe, an ability to navigate in poor weather, having the know-how to deal with the cold, and most importantly, the nous to make good judgement calls when it comes to mountain conditions. This is a set of skills that can be used as a benchmark to measure yourself against; if you are lacking in any of them, take it as sign that you should tag along with someone experienced, at least for your first few outings.

On the whole, it is usual for most parties to climb un-roped in grade I gullies and on the more straightforward ridge traverses. It is still a sensible measure to carry a rope to help deal with anything unexpected; to get past an icy step or a large cornice, to give security to someone having a wobble, or even to keep the entire party together in a whiteout. Whilst knowing how to use a rope in such situations is very handy, on easier routes it is nowhere near as important as being able to move comfortably using an axe and crampons.

Skills and Equipment

For the harder routes, particularly the grade II ridge traverses, most parties head out with the expectation of having to use a rope at some point in the day. A small 'alpine rack' is often carried – a set of nuts, a few hexes, along with three or so long extenders and a few slings – to be able to protect the trickier sections of a route. The range of mountaineering skills needed here is wide and requires knowledge of snow anchors, and the kind of rough-and-ready techniques that are more akin to traditional alpinism than modern rock climbing.

If you're new to the winter mountains, or have little knowledge of when or how a rope could be useful, going on an instructional course makes total sense. Time with a good instructor will never be regretted and lots of people have kick-started their winter mountaineering this way. There are many talented instructors based throughout the Highlands who offer their services on a daily basis.

Equipment Coping with winter in Scotland requires similar clothing and equipment to that used in other cold mountain environments. Most summer hillwalkers and trad climbers living in Britain are already likely to own a fair amount of the necessary clothing. The following notes only give advice on the most important items and are primarily for the benefit of anybody who is new to Scottish winter mountaineering. They might also help as a reminder for those who've been away for a while.

Helmet – There is a blanket acceptance that it is essential to wear a helmet. If you fall, or slip, or something drops from above, all of which are distinctly possible, even on the easiest of routes, a helmet would undoubtedly reduce the risk of a serious head injury.

Principal clothing – A conventional clothing system made up of a number of versatile layers works well in Scotland and is particularly effective at dealing with the huge range of conditions. It is pretty much standard for a waterproof outer-shell to be worn for the entire day and the layers beneath it swapped according to the temperature or level of exertion. Carrying a simple wind-proof or soft-shell jacket adds further versatility and will make life significantly more comfortable. Balaclavas are worn by people who are up to no good; it is not an attractive look. Wear a nice hat.

Spare clothing – Having a spare piece of warm clothing is sound universal practice. However, in Scotland, any clothing that you may need to rely on in an emergency shouldn't contain natural down/feathers. No matter what the claims of the manufacturer, it will eventually 'wet out' and lose all ability to keep you warm. Carrying two pairs of spare gloves is considered the norm.

Boots and crampons – Any rigid and waterproof mountain boot that is properly compatible with a 12-point general mountaineering crampon will be fine for the job. The ideal combination would be an alpine boot in the B2 category (the type that has a little bit of flex or camber to the sole) fitted with a 12-point crampon in the C2 category (preferably the type with a heel clip and plastic toe bail). Winter climbing boots, in the B3 category, are also fine, although their fully rigid soles can be tiring if you're constantly on the move. To ensure dry feet, cover your boots with a calf-length gaiter.

Headtorch – Another absolutely essential piece of equipment. Taking spare batteries is also crucial. Better still; take a spare headtorch, especially if you're on your own. Modern LED torches are incredibly small and light; carrying a spare, or at least one spare among the party, versus the epic that would ensue following a headtorch failure, is a small concession.

Goggles – There needs to be a cast iron forecast for a calm day before leaving these at home. Without them, the effect of wind blown snow can range from an annoying discomfort through to a complete inability to function. Disregard the myth that the cheapest goggles are the best for Scottish winter; there are times when they need be worn all day.

Rope – Even though the majority of parties remain un-roped on grade I terrain, it is still common practice to carry an 'emergency rope'. Used wisely, and in conjunction with just a sling and a krab, it can be a passport for getting out of most unexpected, tricky situations. There is an art in finding the right balance between travelling light and maintaining safety. This is particularly true when it comes to selecting a rope, where the choice can vary so much in weight and usefulness. The longer the rope, the more useful it is. To be at all useful in Scottish winter mountaineering, the length can't really be anything less than 30m. Also, it takes a very adept person to handle an icy rope of less than 9mm diameter with gloved hands. Draw your own conclusions from this.

Skills and Equipment

Given good conditions, it is perfectly feasible that a competent party could complete any of the harder routes in this book entirely un-roped (with the exception of abseils). They may also opt to carry only a lightweight emergency rope, a choice born out of experience. However, most parties heading onto grade II routes will have an expectation of tying onto a rope at some point in the day. In which case, it is best to take something more substantial; a full-weight rope that is designed for winter mountaineering. If the choice is available, the optimal length would be 40m and a manageable diameter would be around 9 to 9.5mm.

Navigation equipment – A smartphone loaded with mapping software will show you exactly where you are on a digital 1:50,000 map. There is no necessity to be within mobile coverage. This is incredibly useful technology; don't question it, just embrace it – OS Maps and Fatmap are probably the two most popular apps and are relatively inexpensive for what they are. OS Locate is free and simply converts GPS location readings from your mobile into grid references. Your smartphone will need to be protected by a waterproof and touch-sensitive cover, and it's wise to also have a back-up power charge.

There are limitations to relying on a smartphone for pinpointing where you are, not least the fragility of electronic equipment. Wild weather can make using a touch screen very difficult and sub-zero temperatures can significantly shorten battery life. A bespoke and more robust GPS unit, with easier to operate control buttons, can go some way to solving these issues. However, the additional cost and no improvement in accuracy means that it does not often warrant a place in most people's rucksacks. Despite its drawbacks, a smartphone in a protective case is the way forward for most hill-goers in Scotland - it can also make calls and send texts!

For proper hands-on navigation - actually finding your way safely across a mountainside in poor visibility - there is no substitute for being able to use a map and compass. In a Scottish blizzard, outsourcing your sense of direction to a small screen just won't cut it. Use your mobile solely as a tool to verify where you are (which is just about practical in most situations), but to get from one location to another, it is best to stick to a map and compass. A Type 4 Silva compass is particularly suited to Scottish conditions; its long base plate is easy to hold, the bezel is easy to operate and it has romers for both OS and Harvey's maps. An old-school wrist altimeter can also be useful.

Group shelter – Also known as a bothy bag. An indispensible item, not only if things go wrong but also as a means of respite on a windy mountainside. These thin nylon shelters are the mainstay of survival equipment for the Scottish mountains. They come in a variety of sizes and are incredibly light; a 2-person shelter can weigh less than 250 grams.

Climbing equipment – What technical gear to take, if any, is an endless debate. There is no correct answer. The route you intend to do, your level of experience and the mountain conditions forecast for the day, will all influence your decision. Consensus is that an 'alpine rack' would be adequate for most parties, regardless of experience – a set of nuts, a few hexes (rather than cams), three or so long extenders and some slings should be all that is needed to protect the stiffer sections of the harder routes in this book. There are no rules; take whatever gear you feel you may need.

Axe – The most versatile length of axe for general Scottish mountaineering is somewhere between 50cm and 55cm. Any longer than 60cm, an axe becomes unwieldy when scrambling or on steep snow, and will also prove difficult to control during an ice axe arrest. A straight or curved shaft is down to personal preference. However, the shaft's diameter needs to be substantial enough to allow a secure grip without the help of a leash. A wide adze is very useful. The stronger 'T' rated construction classification is preferable to 'B' rated.

The current axe of choice for most people is either the high-quality 'Summit Evo' from Petzl or the 'Cirque' from Welsh manufacturer DMM. Surprisingly, the 'Cirque' is DMM's budget model and one of the least expensive mountaineering axes available. While it may have its flaws, its curved geometry is spot on for winter scrambling, as is the reassuring wide diameter of its shaft. And it is weighty enough to instil confidence when conditions are hard going.

For those who prefer a traditional straight shaft, the choice is limited; virtually all straight-shafted axes are now primarily designed with ski touring or glacial travel in mind, which makes them a bit too lightweight for everyday Scottish use. Mountain Technology's mountaineering axes were the epitome of utilitarian design and probably the most suited ever made for biffing around in Scotland's mountains. Sadly the company folded in 2004 but their axes remain popular; they regularly exchange hands via online auctions.

Skills and Equipment

Mountain rescue Cover in Scotland is provided by regionally based volunteer teams. Should you have an accident or get into difficulty in the mountains, the local team will organise a rescue and come to your aid. They offer this service 24 hours a day, all year round and in all weathers. Team members are all experienced mountaineers and regularly give up their time to train in search and rescue techniques. They are professional in the way they operate but are unpaid. Why do they volunteer? Well, there doesn't seem to be any consistent answer. Just take it that they are all part of a wider community who in some way share a connection with the mountains.

Having a team of unknown volunteers prepared to put themselves at risk to help you out seems an extremely one-sided pact. The very least that can be done to rebalance this arrangement is to help make sure that your potential rescuers have the best of kit and the funds to cover their training and operational costs. Teams receive a small part of their funding from the Scottish Government; the remainder has to come from fundraising and donations. Consider making the occasional donation. Individual teams can be supported directly (details on their respective websites), or through Scottish Mountain Rescue, a co-ordinating body for the majority of the teams.

What to do in an emergency In the event of an accident, the first thing to do is pause and take a moment to evaluate the situation rationally. If there is any possibility of limping safely back to the valley under your own steam, this is always the preferable option. If there is no sensible option other than to get help and you are fortunate to have a mobile signal, then call 999 (or 112) and ask for the police. Once connected to the local police, then ask for mountain rescue. If you can't give a grid reference, have ready as much information as possible that could help identify your location and be prepared to calmly explain what has happened. Do exactly as instructed by the rescue team.

At the time of writing, there is mobile coverage across roughly 40% of the mountainous area described in this book. As a rule of thumb, the best signal is likely to be found across the tops and on ridgelines, or when there is line of sight to a road. Areas of no or very poor signal strength are generally within enclosed corries or on mountain flanks facing away from a road. An emergency 999 call will automatically connect through any available network, even when your own provider is displaying no connection.

When the mobile signal is too weak to support a voice call, it may still be possible to send an emergency text. To be able to do this, you need to have registered your phone in advance – text 'register' to 999 and follow the instructions in the reply.

An accident occurring in a remote area, with no mobile signal, is perhaps the scariest scenario. There is often no single course of action that can be taken and you'll likely be faced with multiple options. Only by being familiar with emergency procedures and having good mountaineering nous can you be properly prepared for the very difficult decisions that would undoubtedly ensue. Carrying the previously mentioned safety kit (a group shelter and spare clothing) would be crucial to a happy outcome. The international distress signal of 6 short blasts on a whistle (or flashes from a torch), followed by a minute's silence, may be your only method of attracting assistance.

As a sensible precaution on any mountain journey, a note or digital message with your intended route and estimated return time should be left with a reliable person back at home. A note could also be left in the windscreen of your vehicle, displaying the widely recognised letters EPOC (emergency point of contact) next to the phone number of your reliable friend.

Personal locator beacons (PLB) have only recently been available for use on land in the UK, but despite the obvious safety benefit they provide, their uptake has been negligible. Unlike mobile phones, PLB use seems to cross a philosophical line with many hill-goers in Scotland. Time may change attitudes but at present they are viewed as counter to the very reasons for heading to the hills. Any PLB needs to be registered with the Maritime and Coastguard Agency (MCA), for which there is no charge. If your beacon is activated and a distress signal received by the MCA, the search and rescue authorities will contact your nominated EPOC. You therefore still need to leave details of your intended route with your reliable friend (your EPOC).

Winter mountaineering in Scotland is dangerous. No matter how much care you take, bad stuff can happen. Think about what you could do to look after an injured partner on a cold and windy mountainside. If you're at all unsure of how you would deal with such a situation, consider it another prompt to go on an instructional course, or at least to gain some knowledge of emergency procedures. Good practical advice is available in Kath Wills' comprehensive book *Outdoor First Aid*.

Descending the east ridge of Sgorr Dhonuill on Beinn a' Bheithir - Stormé England

01 Lochnagar The Black Spout

The long approach slopes leading up to the Black Spout - Steve Worth

area
The White Mounth, East Highlands

start
NO 309 851

difficulty
Grade I

distance
16.3km

total ascent
1030m

map
page 26

An atmospheric gully climb in a wild mountain corrie This is a journey into big open country, typical of the East Highlands. With a notably colder and drier climate than mountains elsewhere, the high cliffs and tops of Lochnagar often remain sub-zero while thawing westerlies strip the west coast hills.

When wind is thrown into the mix, the area's colder weather is well known for producing savage spindrift blizzards, making this a testing outing. Stable snow conditions are important, as a number of regular avalanche run-outs are crossed between entering Lochnagar's northeast corrie and gaining the summit plateau. The gully fills with snow early in the season and is resilient to thaws.

Lochnagar The Black Spout

Background The White Mounth is an extensive and sprawling mountainous plateau that lies just south of the river Dee, in the southeast corner of the Cairngorms National Park. It is an area known as Royal Deeside and is, with reasonable certainty, the most comfortable region of the Highlands. The area's valleys and wooded glens are incredibly picturesque but its lower hills are penetrated by the bulldozed tracks of sporting estates and coloured by the patchwork of burnt grouse moor.

In winter, the high ground of the White Mounth shows little submission to intrusion by the estates and is as wild a mountain environment as any elsewhere in Scotland. The plateau's standout feature is the huge northeast corrie situated beneath its highest and most northerly peak, Cac Carn Beag (1155m). The corrie's granite cliffs reach a height of 220m and extend for over 1.5km to encircle a small lonely loch, Lochnagar, which has given its name to cover the entire northern area of the Mounth.

Lochnagar's cliffs are split by a number of prominent gullies, the majority of which are mid-grade climbing routes. However one gully, by far the biggest and most impressive within the corrie, succumbs easily to a single axe approach and is an excellent way to the top of the mountain. This is the Black Spout.

Description Start at the large car park at the Spittal of Glenmuick (NO 309 851), a pay and display (or pay online afterwards). The only approach to the car park is from Ballater on Deeside, from where a 15km-long single-track road is followed S through Glen Muick.

From the car park, walk SW through the wood to just past the Visitor Centre, then turn right and follow a vehicle track NW across the open valley. At a T-junction on the far side of the valley, continue straight ahead into the trees and follow a footpath that heads W from just beyond a derelict building. After 300m the path joins a vehicle track, which leads out of the pinewood and continues up the open hillside beside the Allt-na-Guibhsaich.

A 2.5km steady climb leads to the vehicle track's high point, the Muick-Gelder col (680m), from where a well-cairned path branches off to the left. After approximately 1.2km, leave this path and head NW up to the col between the Meikle Pap (980m) and Cuidhe Cròm (1083m). The col provides the first opportunity to see the northeast corrie and the first view of the distinctive, deep recess of the Black Spout, which splits the cliffs on the opposite side of the loch.

Deep inside the left branch of the Black Spout, with the Glen Muick Hills in the distance - Steve Worth

Lochnagar The Black Spout

Descend leftwards/SW into the corrie. Continue dropping until about 50 metres above the loch, from where it is possible to contour beneath the lowest outcrops of rock that project from the foot of the northeast cliffs. Beyond the outcrops take a direct line NW towards the Black Spout and climb the long approach slopes that lead up to the gully.

Two huge buttresses flank the gully's entrance and set the tone for an atmospheric ascent. From start to finish, the gully is hemmed between steep granite walls, whose sheltering effect can often provide an eerie tranquillity, even on really blustery days. At mid-height the gully forks. Head up the left branch, which is the more scenic and, although steeper, still remains grade I. Any large cornice can always be outflanked (within reason!). From the top of the gully, head NNW for 350m across open ground to Lochnagar's airy summit, Cac Carn Beag (1155m).

Return From the summit cairn head SSE, retracing your steps to the top of the Black Spout. Now follow the cliff edge around the rim of the corrie, passing over a minor top (1078m) before dropping NE down a steep boulder-covered slope. From just below the Meikle Pap col, rejoin the path used on the approach.

In stormy weather, or if easterly winds that were an assistance on the way up are now a pain, head S from any point near the cliff edge. This leads into the upper catchment area of the Glas Allt, which is followed SE, down a good path towards Loch Muick. The path drops steeply alongside an impressive waterfall before zig-zagging down to the lochside. Head NE along the lochside path, then skirt around the northern end of the loch to join a vehicle track that leads N, back to the Spittal of Glenmuick. This is a longer descent route but much less stressful to navigate.

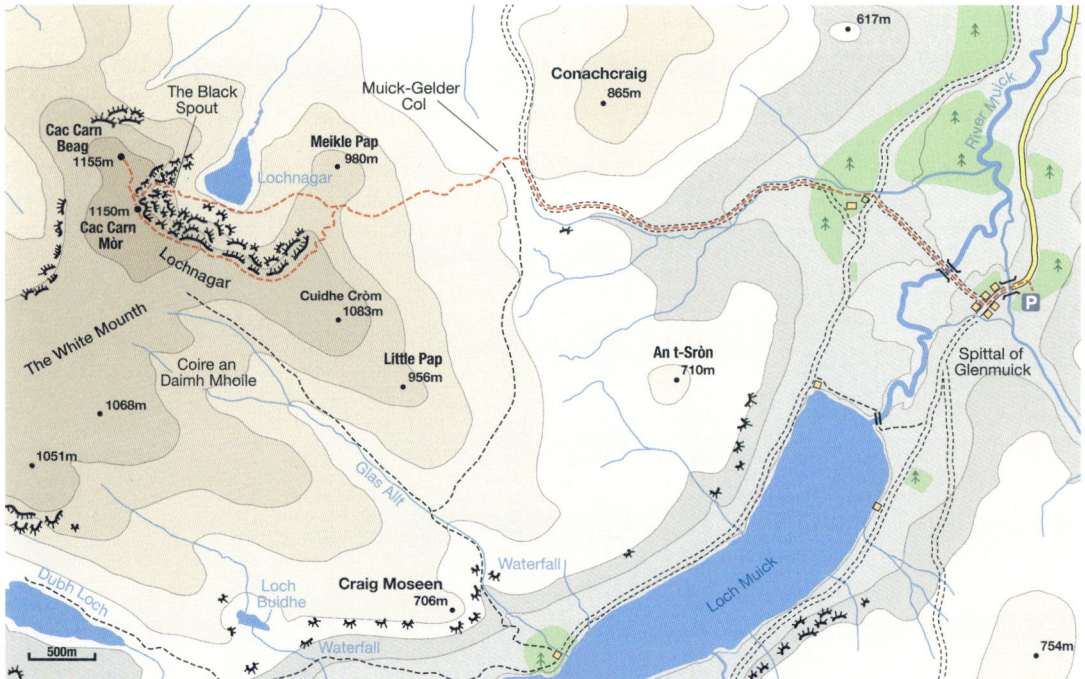

02 Northern Cairngorms Over the Back

Alladin's Seat and the view across Coire an t-Sneachda.
Cold powdery conditions in early January - Adam Fisher

area
Cairngorms,
East Highlands

start
NH 989 060

difficulty
Grade I

distance
12.7km

total ascent
1065m

map
page 31

An adventurous journey 'over the back' to the remote Loch Avon Basin
This long and varied outing travels through vast mountain scenery, linking three of the area's biggest gullies. It is an unusual and intimate way in which to explore the interior of the Northern Cairngorms.

Not the wisest of undertakings if there is any prospect of severe weather. The hazards of returning across the plateau into an oncoming gale do not bear thinking about. Any reduction in visibility gives the potential for some very difficult navigation. It is best reserved for a fairly calm day, when there is stable snow on all aspects.

Northern Cairngorms Over the Back

Background Rather than being considered a range of mountains, the Cairngorms are sometimes thought of as one immense mountain topped by an intricate, rolling plateau. A notion that seems important to some people, especially those who have fallen under the Cairngorm spell. Confusingly, the range's name, or the mountain's name, is borrowed from just one of its many summits, Cairn Gorm.

At its northwest edge, the Cairngorm plateau sits dominantly above the forested slopes of Glen More and Glen Feshie. From here it spreads out in easterly and southerly directions, for up to 30km at its furthest extent. The bulk of the plateau stands above 1000m with a number of its peaks pushing above 1200m. In fact, the plateau supports five of the six highest peaks in Scotland. However, this is a mountain whose character is less about its highest summits and more about the deep-set corries and long glens that carve into its interior. It is a special environment, arctic in scientific classification, or put more emotionally, it is wild and magical.

The ferocity of the storms that cross the plateau is without comparison. A cold continental-like climate and winds that accelerate to frightening speeds through the rolling topography, combine to produce the notorious Cairngorm blizzards. But this is not the only side to the story. When the winds abate and the snows firm, ideal conditions arise for venturing into the mountain's magnificent winter landscape. And this is where this journey goes.

Description Start from the Coire Cas car park at the Cairngorm ski area (NH 989 060). The car park's elevation at 620m makes it a no-brainer as the obvious starting point for any forays into the Northern Cairngorms east of the Lairig Ghru. The ski area is reached by taking the clearly signposted Coylumbridge Road from Aviemore. There are snow gates at Glenmore, just before the road begins its long climb up the hill from Loch Morlich. Occasionally, following strong winds, the gates are closed until the 'ski road', as it is known at this point, can be cleared of snow. The status of the road is regularly updated on social media by the ski area staff.

Head SW from the top of the car park on a well-constructed path, which passes beneath the lowest ski tow before traversing around the hillside to the right/W of the ski area. After 400m, take the left branch at a fork and follow an equally good path S, which climbs gently uphill into Coire an t-Sneachda. The path peters out at a boulder field that extends across the corrie floor. Veer slightly to the E and pick the easiest way through the boulders to reach the snow apron beneath the corrie headwall.

In the middle of the headwall, where the cliff base is at its lowest, is an obvious, steep dome-shaped mass of rock, topped by an 8m-high pinnacle. This is Aladdin's Buttress. To the left of the buttress is the entrance to a long dog-leg shaped gully, Alladin's Couloir, the first gully of the journey (NH 994 031).

Returning across the Cairngorm Plateau with alpine conditions in late March - Stevie Butterworth

A clearing squall reveals the huge cliffs of Shelterstone Crag - Karen McIntyre

The initial part of the gully is straightforward. In lean conditions, ice may form at the narrows before the gully bends to the right. The ice never extends above the narrows and does not increase the grade. Beyond the bend the gully widens and continues easily up to a narrow col level with Aladdin's Seat, the 8m-high pinnacle. A steep snow slope now leads to the plateau, with any cornice normally being out-flanked on the right.

From the top of Aladdin's couloir head SE across the plateau, aiming for an area of flat headland overlooking the Loch Avon basin. On the southern periphery of the flattening are two gullies that drop steeply towards the head of the basin. The left-hand or more easterly gully is Diagonal Gully (NJ 001 022), the second gully of the journey. Its identity can be confirmed by the distinctive mosaic pattern on the rocks just below its top.

Bail straight down the gully, which is at its steepest near the top. The gully is long and particularly atmospheric in descent… like dropping into another world. In its lower reaches, the angle eases off sufficiently to allow a good bum-slide if snow conditions are favourable.

From the snow apron beneath the gully, head SSW towards the large boulder field on the far side of the glen. If crossing the Fèith Buidhe is problematic, move upstream to just above the first fork, where the burn is braided and can likely be hopped across. A cairn marks one of the biggest boulders. This is the famous Shelter Stone; a large natural hollow beneath the boulder has been made weather tight and provides reasonable shelter for up to six people.

Dropping into Diagonal Gully and the depths of the Loch Avon basin - Scott Brooks

Northern Cairngorms Over the Back
Northern Cairngorms The Fiacaill Ridge

Northern Cairngorms Over the Back

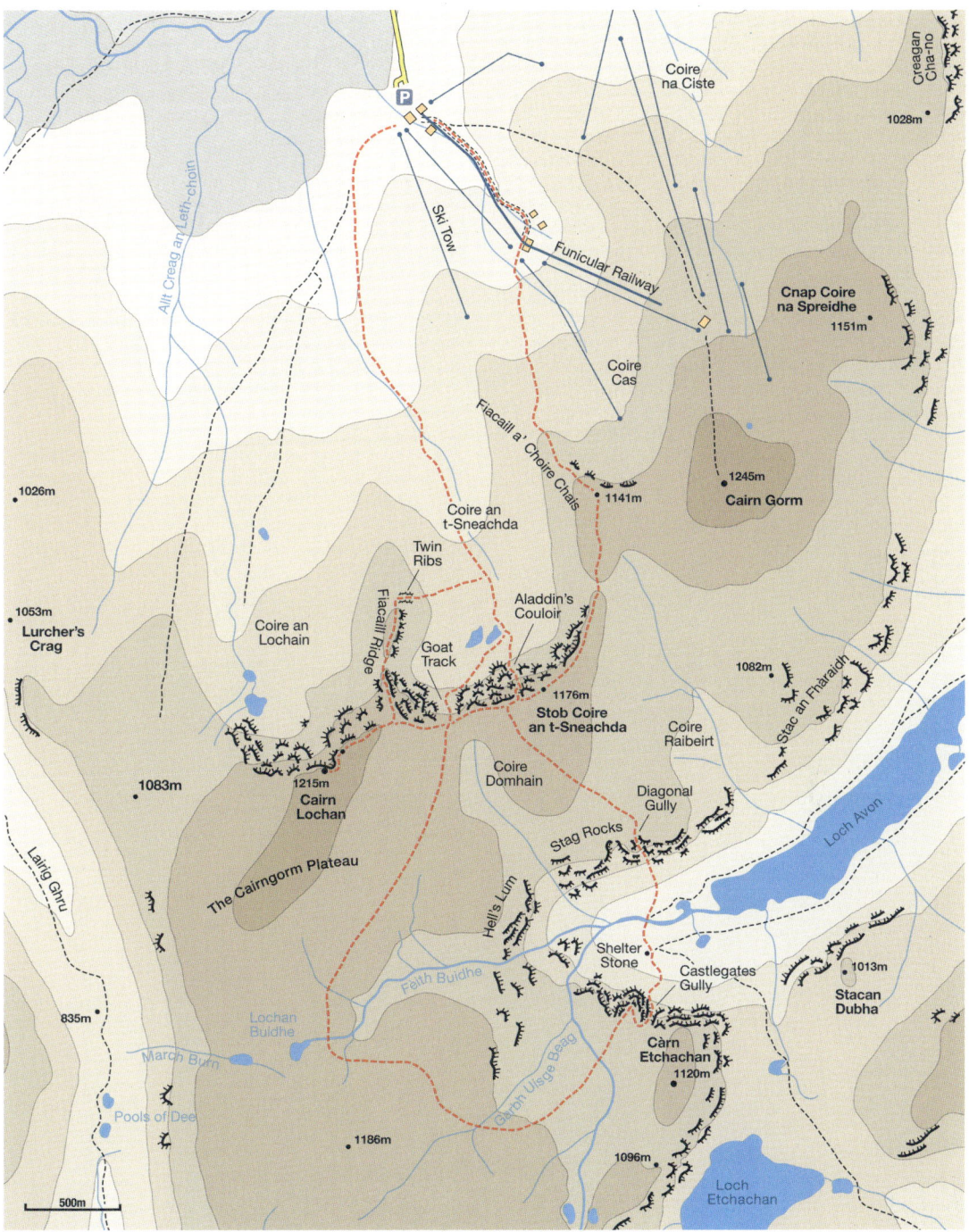

Northern Cairngorms Over the Back

Towering above the boulder field are the huge cliffs of Shelter Stone Crag and Càrn Etchachan. Separating these two great cliffs, but hidden from view, is the third gully of the journey, the aptly named Castlegates Gully. From the highest point on the boulder field take a rising leftward line to reach the gully's entrance at the apex of the snow apron (NJ 002 012). The gully is much easier-angled than Diagonal or Aladdin's and the ascent is uncomplicated. From its top, head 125m NNW to reach the flat-topped summit of Shelterstone Crag and a fine central spot from which to survey the whole of the Loch Avon Basin.

Return coming back across the plateau is perhaps the most demanding part of the journey. Head initially SW before curving to the NW, contouring around the catchment areas of the Garbh Uisge Beag and the Fèith Buidhe. Both streams are likely to be safely buried in a freeze but can be lurking under thin snow bridges late in the season. Beyond the depression of the Fèith Buidhe, and having ascended to around 1140m, contour to the NE aiming to arrive at the broad col at the head of Coire Domhain (1111m).

A cairn at the centre of the col marks the top of the Goat Track, the summer path dropping N into Coire an t-Sneachda. The path, a long grade I snow slope in winter, provides the quickest and most sheltered route back to the car park. It is a common descent route for teams climbing in the corrie and late in the day is likely to have a track. With conditions still permitting, bail directly down the slope. After dropping 50m or so, veer to the true right and continue descending by an obtuse line beneath the cliffs of the corrie headwall. At the corrie floor, cross the boulder field and regain the approach path.

For the staying-high return route, ascend NE from the col at the head of Coire Domhain and follow the corrie rim over Stob Coire an t-Sneachda (1176m), around to spot height 1141m; an unmistakable 2m-high boulder crowned with a cairn. From '1141', as it is commonly abbreviated to, descend NW down the Fiacaill a' Choire Chais. Either continue on this line to the bottom of the ski area or break off right when appropriate, aiming for the vehicle track on the far side of the funicular halfway station. Be considerate to skiers and avoid walking on the groomed pistes.

Approaching the hidden entrance to Castlegates Gully - Karen McIntyre, Heather Morning, Sarah Crowsely and Fiona Weatherall

Biting spindrift in Castelgates Gully - Scott Brooks

03 Northern Cairngorms The Fiacaill Ridge

The Fiacaill Ridge on a wild Cairngorm day - Kath James

area
Cairngorms,
East Highlands

start
NH 989 060

difficulty
Grade I/II

distance
8.6km

total ascent
720m

map
page 31

A first rate winter ridge This is a short but thoroughly satisfying journey, with quality winter scrambling and vast, spacious views. The convenient approach from the ski area car park makes for an ideal half-day hit. It can be attempted in any snow conditions and is safe from avalanche.

Although this is a justifiably popular route, it is still relatively easy not to encounter other teams. The windy nature of the Northern Corries tends to 're-set' the ridge's appearance each night; snow is re-distributed, tracks disappear and the rime ice is re-grown. An early start may give that magical un-touched element to the climb, which is always quite special in the Cairngorms.

Northern Cairngorms The Fiacaill Ridge

Background The Northern Corries of the Cairngorms sit along the northwest edge of the plateau, overlooking Loch Morlich and the Rothiemurchus Forest. Their high elevation and northerly aspect, combined with the Cairngorms' cold climate, ensures they are among the earliest recipients of the winter season's snow. With the exception of the more remote corries tucked away in the plateau's interior, they also have the most long-lasting and reliable snow cover in Scotland.

There are three principal corries, the most easterly of which, Coire Cas, is situated directly beneath Cairn Gorm (1244m) and is home to the main ski area. The central corrie, Coire an t-Sneachda, is the most attractive for mountaineering, with a long, impressive headwall peppered with an excellent selection of easy gully lines. Immediately to the west is Coire an Lochain, whose compact cirque of buttresses, with their steep approach slopes, give the corrie a serious feel.

Coire an t-Sneachda and Coire an Lochain are separated by a long whale-backed ridge; the Fiacaill of Coire an t-Sneachda, more commonly known as just the Fiacaill Ridge. Beyond its broad top, as it nears the plateau, the ridge becomes well-defined then quickly steepens. Here the crest is topped by granite tors and blocks, which offer thoughtful winter scrambling in a dramatic and airy position. It is a ridge you are likely to 'nip up' on more than one occasion.

Description Start from the Coire Cas car park at the Cairngorm ski area (NH 989 060). The car park's elevation at 620m makes it a no-brainer as the obvious starting point for any forays into the Northern Cairngorms east of the Lairig Ghru. The ski area is reached by taking the clearly signposted Coylumbridge Road from Aviemore. There are snow gates at Glenmore, just before the road begins its long climb up the hill from Loch Morlich. Occasionally, following strong winds, the gates are closed until the 'ski road', as it is known at this point, can be cleared of snow. The status of the road is regularly updated on social media by the ski area staff.

Head SW from the top of the car park on a well-constructed path that passes beneath the lowest ski tow before traversing around the hillside to the right/W of the ski area. After 400m, take the left branch at a fork and follow an equally good path S, which climbs gently uphill into Coire an t-Sneachda.

The Fiacaill Ridge bounds the right-hand side of the corrie and from the approach appears as a large pyramidal hill. Dropping down from its apex, towards the corrie floor, are two ill-defined rocky ribs; the Twin Ribs. Continue up the path until a noticeable flattening of the corrie floor at around 920m. Then break W, directly towards the base of the ribs, which are located a short way up the hillside (NH 989 036). Even using a GPS, finding the ribs in poor visibility can be a complete bugger.

The Fiacaill of Coire an t-Sneachda from the corrie path. The Twin Ribs visible just below the left-hand skyline - Dave Lees

Northern Cairngorms The Fiacaill Ridge

The right-hand rib is the more continuous of the two and its crest provides a good and objectively safe winter scrambling line onto the Fiacaill. Gain the distinctive notch just above the rib's truncated base. In suspect snow conditions this is best approached from the right, avoiding the deep convex snowfield directly beneath the rib. From the notch, pick the most appealing way to the top of the rib, which is much better than it looks from the corrie floor.

Head S, without any difficulty, up the broad shoulder of the Fiacaill and over its summit. Optional, easy scrambling along the tops of small buttresses adds exposure and fun. Just beyond a level section, the ridge rears up dramatically with the steep cliffs of the Fiacaill Buttress forming its left-hand side. Climb directly up a recess in the centre of the ridge to gain a flattening on the crest above. This crux section can be avoided by skirting around its base to the right/W, to then climb a tight little corner before cutting up left over blocky steps to reach the flattening. Continue up the ridge, sticking to the crest as closely as is sensible.

If visibility is good, it is well worth making the short detour onto Cairn Lochan (1215m) for the big country views over Braeriach and the Sgòrans. From where the Fiacaill Ridge merges into the plateau, veer SW up featureless slopes leading onto a large flat area above the cliffs of Coire an Lochain. The indistinguishable summit is the more westerly of two cairns, just beyond a corniced recess.

Return From the summit of Cairn Lochan, head ENE down easy slopes to reach the broad col at the head of Coire Domhain (1111m). A cairn at the centre of the col marks the top of the Goat Track, the summer path dropping N into Coire an t-Sneachda. The path, a long grade I snow slope in winter, provides the quickest and most sheltered route back to the car park. It is a common descent route for teams climbing in the corrie and late in the day is likely to have a track.

If this is a safe conditions day with little avalanche risk, bail directly down the slope. After dropping 50m or so, veer to the true-right and continue descending by an obtuse line beneath the cliffs of the corrie headwall. At the corrie floor, cross the boulder field and head down the centre of the corrie, which is the line of the path leading to the ski area car park.

If there are unstable snow conditions, or simply to stay high, ascend NE from the col at the head of Coire Domhain and follow the corrie rim over Stob Coire an t-Sneachda (1176m), around to spot height 1141m; an unmistakable 2m-high boulder crowned with a cairn. From '1141', as it is commonly abbreviated to, descend NW down the Fiacaill a' Choire Chais. Either continue on this line to the bottom of the ski area or break off right when appropriate, aiming for the vehicle track on the far side of the Funicular halfway station. Be considerate to skiers and avoid walking on the groomed pistes.

Northern Cairngorms The Fiacaill Ridge

Quality shizzling along the blocky crest of the Fiacaill Ridge - Sheila van Lieshout

The first team on the ridge as early morning light hits the Fiacaill Buttress

04 An Teallach The Ridge Traverse

Ascending Sgùrr Fiona in deep snow, two days after a mid-March storm - Keith and Anne Robertson

area
Dundonnell, Northwest Highlands

start
NH 114 850

difficulty
Grade II

distance
15.1km

total ascent
1450m

map
page 40

A magnificent outing and perhaps the embodiment of Scottish winter mountaineering A beautiful ridge that when combined with the right day, and the right company, can give the most magical mountain experience. It is a long and committing undertaking, requiring a realistic level of winter hill fitness. The need for a decent forecast is a given.

An Teallach is a high mountain and frequently in good winter condition. However, figuring how easy the going will be is a complicated affair. Too much snow can make the approach time-consuming. Conversely, a build-up on the tops can make the crossing of Corrag Bhuidhe's pinnacles (the crux) technically easier. Then again, powder or unconsolidated snow can be extremely taxing when climbing over the rounded summit blocks. Just go with it, expect the unexpected and make the right decisions.

An Teallach The Ridge Traverse

Background An Teallach sits in the northwest corner of the wide mountainous expanse often referred to as the Great Wilderness; an uninhabited area that stretches from Little Loch Broom in the north to Loch Maree in the south. It is a huge mountain with many peaks, and whose distinctive skyline seems to invoke a universal emotional response; a longing for the Scottish hills. The iconic view from An Teallach's highest point, looking out across its southern tops, has come to symbolise Scottish winter mountaineering.

An Teallach is essentially a double horseshoe-shaped ridge that encloses two large, east-facing corries. Two subsidiary ridges project out to the north and west, extending the mountain's footprint by over 3km in both directions. The majority of the mountain's peaks are located around the southern corrie, Toll an Lochain. It is this line of peaks, with their long, narrow, serrated crest, that form the mountain's classic ridge traverse.

The highest part of the crest is at its northern end and is made up of two Munros, Bidein a' Ghlas Thuill (1062m) and Sgùrr Fiona (1060m). However, the central part of the crest is the more impressive; a series of exposed sandstone towers and pinnacles known as Corrag Bhuidhe. In winter the traverse is best done from south to north; there is less tricky down-climbing, route finding is easier and there is a superb peak on which to finish.

Description Start at a layby near Corrie Hallie on the A832, 4.3km southeast of Dundonnell (NH 114 850). From 50m S of the layby, head SW along the Shenavall track. After 3km, just beyond the track's highest point, a small path breaks off to the right and heads SW towards Shenavall Bothy. Follow the path for approximately 1.5km to just beyond a stream, the Allt Lochan na Bràthan. Now strike W over open ground and start the long ascent of Sàil Liath (954m), the best line depending on snow conditions.

From Sàil Liath's rounded summit, drop NW into a long col (a minor top rises incongruously from its midpoint), then climb easily up to the more shapely Stob Cadha Gobhlach (960m). From here, head N down gentle slopes before veering NW and dropping more steeply into a lower col (833m). Climb NNW out of the col, up straightforward snow slopes, to reach a shoulder with a rocky crest. This is the top of the south buttress of Corrag Bhuidhe (946m), which drops dramatically to the corrie floor. The shoulder is also the beginnings of a ridge leading up to the first of Corrag Bhuidhe's pinnacles (1042m).

Lord Berkeley's Seat, the overhanging pinnacle marking the end of Corrag Bhuidhe, with the Fisherfield mountains in the distance - Sheila van Lieshout

An Teallach The Ridge Traverse

Climbing the ridge can be the crux of the traverse and requires a steady approach. It is particularly unnerving near the top, where a groove to the right, above the void, is the best line. An easier alternative is to go up the ridge for about 30m and then traverse left along a terrace. When beneath the first feasible looking line, cut back and climb up to the crest of the pinnacles. Continuing along the terrace (a path in summer) will miss out the majority of the difficulties but will still be at least grade I. On occasions the terrace banks-out and may not offer a safer alternative route.

The crest of the pinnacles is very exposed and route finding involves some sniffing around, but is, in most parts, obvious. Generally, the crest can be followed for the majority of the time, with a little bit of side-shuffling to bypass the odd steep step. Down-climbing sections are often much easier on the left/southwest flank.

Following on from the final, squat pinnacle, an easy slope drops down to Lord Berkeley's seat (1030m); a spectacular prow-shaped buttress that overhangs Toll an Lochain. An ascent is optional, otherwise sidle across easy-angled slopes on the southwest flank, which lead to a narrow col just beyond the buttress. A steep but straightforward ridge then climbs directly up to Sgùrr Fiona (1060m), An Teallach's second highest summit.

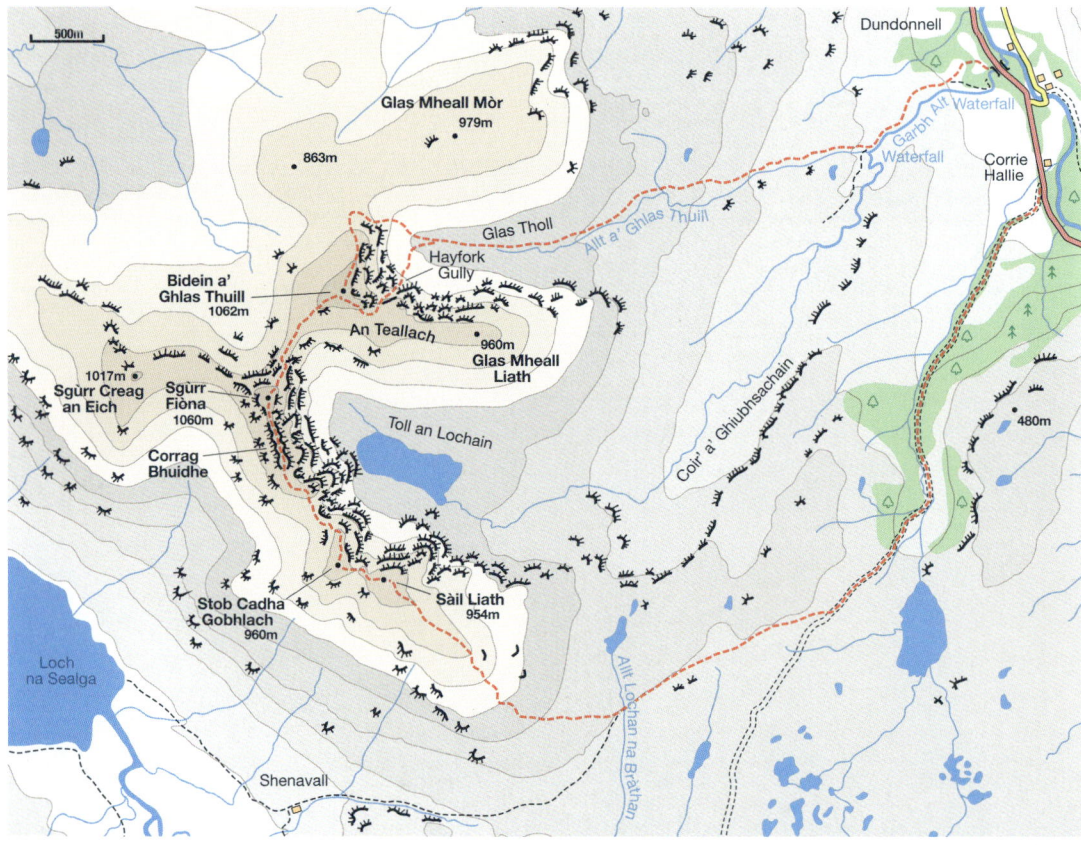

An Teallach The Ridge Traverse
An Teallach Hayfork Gully

Caught in a sudden squall on Corrag Bhuidhe's pinnacles - Sheila van Lieshout

An Teallach The Ridge Traverse

From the summit, descend NE, initially down a steep snow slope that quickly converges into a fine arête. In poor visibility be conscious of the need to veer to the NW at 950m (height), away from the arête. This avoids a false line (the arête drops abruptly into Toll an Lochain) and will place you safely onto the long and narrow col that connects to Bidein a' Ghlas Thuill, An Teallach's highest peak. From the far end of the col, climb NNE up a straightforward slope to the mountain's sharp summit and the most iconic view in the Highlands.

Return Head down the narrow NNE ridge of Bidein a' Ghlas Thuill, towards the plateau at the head of Glas Tholl. Where the ridge markedly steepens, it becomes easier to continue on the left/W flank by scrambling down through short walls and ledges. From the plateau the descent into Glas Tholl is frequently barred by a cornice, which can extend around the whole western lip of the corrie. If problematic, down-climbing at the far right (on the true-right) is usually best, close to the cliffs beneath Bidein á Ghlas Thuill.

Continue down the centre of the corrie floor and pick up a rough path on the north side of the stream. The path meanders ENE down a shallow ravine and through small sandstone bluffs to meet with the better Toll an Lochain path, near the upper Garbh Allt waterfall. This in turn leads down the northwest bank of the burn, the Allt Coir' a' Ghiubhsachain. A series of small cairns mark the way down through a succession of sandstone terraces and then to the edge of a pine wood and dense rhododendron thicket.

The trick now, especially in fading light, is not to plough into the thicket. Instead, skirt N around its edge, passing beneath a prominent pine-covered knoll, to reach a deer fence. Follow the fence E until a large clearing. A hole in the thicket at the far end of the clearing leads to a small burn. Cross the burn and continue through the break in the rhododendrons to reach the main stream, which is then followed for a few metres to the road. Good luck. A 700m walk S along the road takes you back to Corrie Hallie.

Crossing Sàil Liath at the start of the ridge traverse.
Good snow cover in early March - Sheila van Lieshout

05 An Teallach Hayfork Gully

The steep exit to Hayfork Gully, with lean conditions in early February - Kath James

area
Dundonnell, Northwest Highlands

start
NH 111 858

difficulty
Grade I/II

distance
10.3km

total ascent
1060m

map
page 40

An enchanting climb with probably the best top-out to any gully in Scotland This is a journey into the heart of An Teallach and an extraordinary way to reach the top of the mountain. It is shorter and far less serious than a traverse of the main ridge.

An ascent of Hayfork is likely to be straightforward and without any cornice issues. It is steep and in most conditions will be grade I. However, when lean, the difficulty can jump a grade. The gully is deep and holds snow well. It is a good objective for a late season, alpine-type day, when it may be one of the few places on the mountain to require an axe.

An Teallach Hayfork Gully

Background An Teallach's serrated skyline is perhaps one of the most recognisable in Scotland. And a winter traverse along its crest, as described in route 4, is one of the country's best known mountaineering routes. Less well known is the long, deep gully that sneaks up to within a few hundred metres of the mountain's highest peak, Bidein a' Ghlas Thuill (1062m). This is Hayfork Gully, a 320m cleft of the type unique to Torridonian sandstone mountains.

The gateway to Hayfork is through Glas Tholl, the northernmost of An Teallach's two large, east-facing corries. It is the more modest corrie, still impressive by any standards, but overshadowed by its magnificent neighbour, Toll an Lochain. Both corries dominate the horizon when seen from the A832 as it crosses the moorland between Braemore and Dundonnell. This is the normal approach road to the mountain.

Hayfork is tucked away in the southwest corner of Glas Tholl. Its entrance is unremarkable and gives no indication of the gully's true size. Only when inside Hayfork's lower reaches does its enormity become apparent. A huge vertical wall looms over the central section, adding to the gully's eerie architectural ambience. There are only a handful of gullies like this in the Scottish mountains; of an awe-inspiring scale that humble the visitor. Make sure you climb at least one of them.

Description Start at a small bridge on the A832 (NH 111 858), at a point opposite Dundonnell House. This is 3.6km southeast of Dundonnell and 400m northwest of the turn-off to Badralloch. There is a small parking place adjacent to the bridge. The most recent OS map shows a path starting on the south side of the burn. Ignore this, as an impenetrable rhododendron thicket and problems crossing the burn have made the path's initial stage too difficult to follow.

Instead, follow the north bank of the burn into the thicket. A few metres in, by a low concrete retaining wall, turn right and cross a subsidiary burn. Follow the break through the thicket into a clearing with a deer fence on the right. Follow the deer fence until level with a pine-covered knoll on the left. Head S beneath the knoll, to meet with the original path marked on the map.

Head up the path, following small cairns that mark the way through a succession of sandstone terraces. Continue to where the stream coming from Glas Tholl meets the main burn, just before a large waterfall. From here, follow a smaller path that heads W up the hillside. The path stays to the north side of the stream, the Allt a' Ghlas Thuill, and climbs slowly through small sandstone bluffs before reaching easier ground leading into the corrie.

In the deep central section of Hayfork Gully, with Glas Mheall Liath illuminated behind - Kath James

The layout of the corrie is best surveyed from its western end. From here the complexities of its south bounding cliffs can be interpreted face on and Hayfork Gully easily identified. Scanning from left to right, a row of narrow, parallel snow gullies are the first notable feature. These are the Prongs. Next is a large formidable buttress split by a conspicuous deep gully, the Alley. Moving right by 175m, and much higher up the snow apron, is the unremarkable entrance to Hayfork Gully. Further right again, beyond a large flat-faced buttress, is the narrow entrance to North Gully. Beyond North Gully the cliffs curve rightwards to form an imposing steep wall that bounds the western end of the corrie.

Approaching the entrance to Hayfork (NH 072 844) is underwhelming, but this is short lived. The gully soon opens out to reveal impressive rock architecture, on a staggering scale. Near its top, the gully splits into two forks. The right branch is more scenic and easier, steep but still grade I. The left branch just makes grade II. In lean conditions the right branch becomes a stiff grade II with a mixed step, whilst the left branch maintains its grade and becomes the easier option. Neither branch has a cornice, or at least one that will be a problem.

The branches of Hayfork Gully finish either side of a small peak, which sits in a notch on the southeast ridge of Bidein a' Ghlas Thuill. Head NW up the ridge, sidling across the southwest flank of an intervening small top. From the notch beyond the top, ascend directly to the summit blocks and climb up to the trig point.

Return Head down the narrow NNE ridge of Bidein a' Ghlas Thuill, towards the plateau at the head of Glas Tholl. Where the ridge markedly steepens it becomes easier to continue on the left/W flank, by scrambling down through short walls and ledges. From the plateau the descent into Glas Tholl is frequently barred by a cornice, which can extend around the whole western lip of the corrie. If problematic, down-climbing at the far right (on the true-right) is usually best, close to the cliffs beneath Bidein á Ghlas Thuill.

From the corrie floor, retrace the approach route. In fading light or darkness, care is needed at the rhododendron thicket to avoid a thrash-fest. Take time to identify the best way through.

Battered by sprindrift while heading for the east ridge of Bidein a' Ghlas Thuill - Steve Worth

An Teallach Hayfork Gully

Topping-out to views across Toll an Lochain towards Sgùrr Fiona and Corrag Bhuidhe - Kath James

Entering the magnificent lower reaches of Hayfork Gully, with a substantial build-up of snow in late January - Steve Worth

06 Beinn Eighe The Black Carls

On the crest of the Black Carls in a bitterly cold easterly wind - Martyn Eade and Toby Keep

area
Torridon, Northwest Highlands

start
NH 025 610

difficulty
Grade I

distance
10km

total ascent
960m

map
page 49

A nice little mountaineering circuit that feels like something much bigger
This is a pleasant stroll along a snowy ridge enlivened by just the right amount of exhilarating scrambling. And all in a grand mountain setting. The short duration of any difficulties and a straightforward descent, make it a possible objective for a time-pressed day.

The highlight of the journey is the crossing of the Black Carls, a succession of shattered quartzite pinnacles that sit on the narrow ridge leading up to Sgùrr nan Fhir Duibhe (963m). The ridge is barely 200m in length but appreciable drops to the west and long snowy slopes to the east give it the big feel. Although technically never demanding, a couple of cheeky steps keep it from being a pushover. Fresh snow or powder can slow proceedings more than might be expected.

Beinn Eighe The Black Carls

Background Beinn Eighe, Liathach and Beinn Alligin are rightly regarded as one of the most dramatic and spectacular group of mountains in Scotland. They are ancient; amongst the oldest hills in Britain. And as far from ordinary as it gets. Beinn Eighe is the easternmost of these Torridonian giants, stretching for 7km along the north side of Glen Torridon. It is a huge, sprawling mountain that is best characterised by the sweeping, quartzite covered ridges connecting its numerous tops.

The eastern end of Beinn Eighe, overlooking Kinlochewe, is the snowiest corner of the Torridonian mountains, being the furthest from the sea. Here the peaks of Sgùrr nan Fhir Duibhe and Creag Dhubh are often snow covered to a low level, when the higher and more westerly Beinn Alligin may barely have a white summit. It is the ease of access onto these two fine snowy peaks, combined with the exciting crossing of their short connecting ridge, that makes for such a great wee journey. Wee only on a Torridonian scale that is!

Description Start at the vehicle track that runs past Cairn Sheil (NH 025 610), a small holiday bungalow on the A896 in Glen Torridon, approximately 800m south of Kinlochewe. There are parking places 150m further S at a layby, adjacent to the bridge crossing the Allt á Chuirn. Follow the track W for 500m until it takes a sharp right turn. A few metres beyond the turn, a small cairn marks the beginning of a stalker's path, which heads W towards Beinn Eighe. Follow the well-made path along the north bank of the river and through the remnants of old Caledonian woodland.

After 2km of contemplative walking, the path arrives at a confluence within a small picturesque ravine. This will be the last sheltered spot on a windy day. Drop into the ravine and ford the right-hand/northern stream. A steep scramble then leads onto the spur separating the two streams. A good path on the crest of the spur continues WSW across open moorland, directly towards the prominent east ridge of Creag Dhubh.

The triangular base of the ridge consists of a scattering of small buttresses interspersed by grade I snow slopes. Snow conditions on the day will determine the most efficient route to gain the crest (if visible, the summer path can be followed around to the right flank before weaving up a steep slope of fine quartzite scree). The crest leads directly to Creag Dhubh's northern summit (909m). The tiny summit dome may only have a prominence of some 15m above its immediate surroundings but it feels like, and has the outlook of, a major Highland peak.

Sgùrr nan Fhir Duibhe, with the pinnacles of the Black Carls forming the left-hand skyline

Amble SW along Beinn Eighe's main ridge, passing over Creag Dhubh's blunt southern summit (930m) before arriving at a distinct, rocky step. This is the beginning of the Black Carls. Crossing the pinnacles is very much a 'follow your nose' affair. Weaving along their tops is exposed but never too tricky. There is little scope for deviation onto the flanks. The final pinnacle abuts directly onto the shapely summit of Sgùrr nan Fhir Duibhe (963m).

Return Head ESE, down straightforward, uniform slopes. After dropping 350m the slopes ease off and lead onto a narrow spur, which projects eastwards around the southern periphery of Coire Domhain. Walk along the level spur to its end and then continue in the same direction down gentle slopes onto open moorland. Cross a deer fence at its northern end, at a point just before it begins to dip into the Allt á Chuirn watercourse. Ford the river where possible then scamper up the north bank to reach the stalker's path… and so to Glen Torridon.

The day can be extended by continuing W from Sgùrr nan Fhir Duibhe, along Beinn Eighe's sensational main ridge. Airy yet easy ridge walking leads over Sgùrr Bàn (970m) then continues without any complication to Spidean Coire nan Clach (993m), one of Beinn Eighe's two Munros and the highest point on the ridge.

To descend, drop SW onto a narrow shoulder with a trig point at its far end (977m). From the trig point, drop SSE towards the pronounced spur of the Stùc Coire an Laoigh. From the level section of the Stùc, bail E down easy snow slopes into Coire an Laoigh, or continue descending the spur. Either way will pick up the footpath that meanders down the east bank of the corrie's stream, the Allt Coire an Laoigh. The path arrives at the Glen Torridon road below a small pine plantation (NG 977 578), 6.5km from the start point. Hitching always seems a reliable option on the glen road.

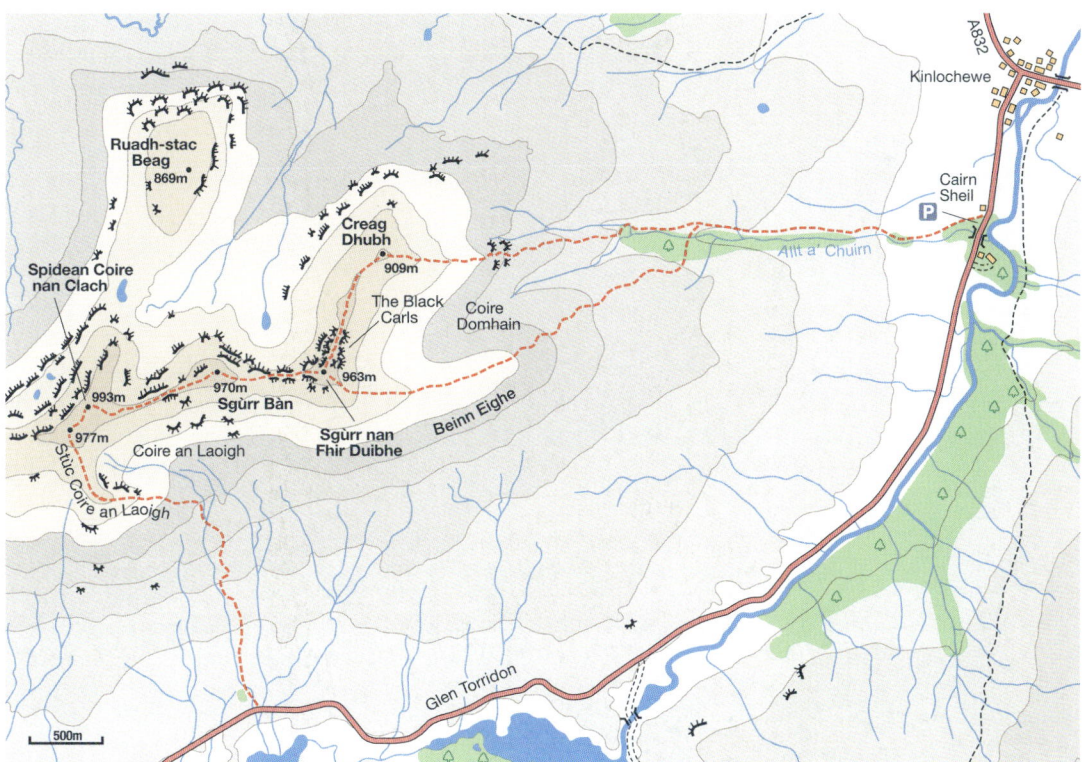

07 Beinn Eighe Morrison's Gully

Climbing Morrison's Gully during an extended cold, dry period in early January - James and Adam Fisher

area
Torridon,
Northwest Highlands

start
NG 957 568

difficulty
Grade I

distance
12.8km

total ascent
1130m

map
page 52

One of the great gullies of the Northwest An incredibly scenic journey that climbs the 360m cleft splitting the north flank of Sail Mhòr (980m), the most impressive of Beinn Eighe's peaks. And from whose summit, the panorama is about as sublime as it gets.

The ascent of Morrison's is usually straightforward. A departure from this is when the snow is bullet-hard. This is an exceptionally long gully, so if it is difficult to kick a step, by the time the steep exit slopes are reached, the going can feel distinctly precarious. With the majority of the gully receiving no direct sunlight, there is often climbable snow until very late in the season.

Beinn Eighe Morrison's Gully

Background The southern flanks of Beinn Eighe, above Glen Torridon, are steep with few features and are covered with uninviting quartzite scree. The north side of the mountain is, however, starkly different. Here a series of long spurs extend out from the main ridge, between which are three remote corries. The westernmost of these corries, Coire Mhic Fhearchair, is widely thought of as one of Scotland's most beautiful, and is somewhere really special.

Coire Mhic Fhearchair is a 'must see' corrie, for a whole host of reasons, not least the Triple Buttress; the huge barrel-shaped cliffs that dominate the rear of the corrie. There is also the view outwards from the corrie mouth, across a landscape so vast that it can create an overwhelming feeling of insignificance. Even though it is a place of pilgrimage for those who love the Scottish mountains, Coire Mhic Fhearchair never sees large numbers of visitors in the winter months. And if it did, you would be unaware, it is of a scale that would swallow them up.

The west side of the corrie is encircled by a narrow spur, which connects the main bulk of Beinn Eighe to the satellite peak of Sail Mhòr. The peak's isolated, prow-shaped summit is perhaps Torridon's best-kept secret. It has a commanding position that overlooks the meeting place of the Torridonian mountains and is set up for surveying the entire length of the hinterland. Climb it.

Description Start at the small car park on the A896 in Glen Torridon (NG 957 568), just W of the bridge crossing the Allt á Choire Dhuibh Mhòir. Follow the footpath up into Coire Dubh Mòr and around the east end of Liathach. At the watershed, near a small, elongated lochan, take a right fork in the path and contour N around Sail Mhòr. The path passes directly beneath Morrisons Gully before climbing slowly up to the sandstone escarpment that forms the lip of Coire Mhic Fhearchair.

From the lip of the corrie, contour W to reach the entrance of Morrison's and climb straight up the atmospheric gully without difficulty. The top of the gully opens out into a steep-sided scoop. Either continue straight up, through broken ground directly towards the summit or, just as good, break out right onto a broad promontory and follow it to the top of Sail Mhòr.

From the summit, strike out across the long, elegant saddle that connects with Còinneach Mhòr (976m); the plateau-topped peak above the Triple Buttress. Sitting high up at the far end of the saddle, and blocking access onto the plateau, is a squat buttress. The buttress can be climbed more or less directly at grade II. Alternatively, contour around to the right, before cutting back left and scrambling up to a recess. The recess is steep but offers an easier route, grade I, onto the crest of the buttress, which is then followed over slabby steps to the summit plateau.

Early morning at Coire Mhic Fhearchair, looking out towards Baosbheinn and Beinn an Eòin - James and Adam Fisher

Beinn Eighe Morrison's Gully

Return From the summit cairn of Còinneach Mhòr, head E, gently downhill, for approximately 800m. This will bring you to a flattening with a re-entrant (a depression in the ground), biting in from the right/south (NG 952 598). Go too far and the ground begins to rise again, up to a pronounced 20m-high mound marking the start of the narrow sweeping ridge that connects to Spidean Coire nan Clach (993m).

To descend to the glen, choose the most favourable looking point anywhere on the flattening and bail obliquely downhill in a SSE direction (steep!). This trajectory will ultimately collide with a distinctive furrow or streambed. At the furrow, head downhill, sticking initially to the right bank. Exceptionally long bum-slides are often possible. Cross the floor of the glen to meet with the Coire Dubh Mòr path… and so to Glen Torridon.

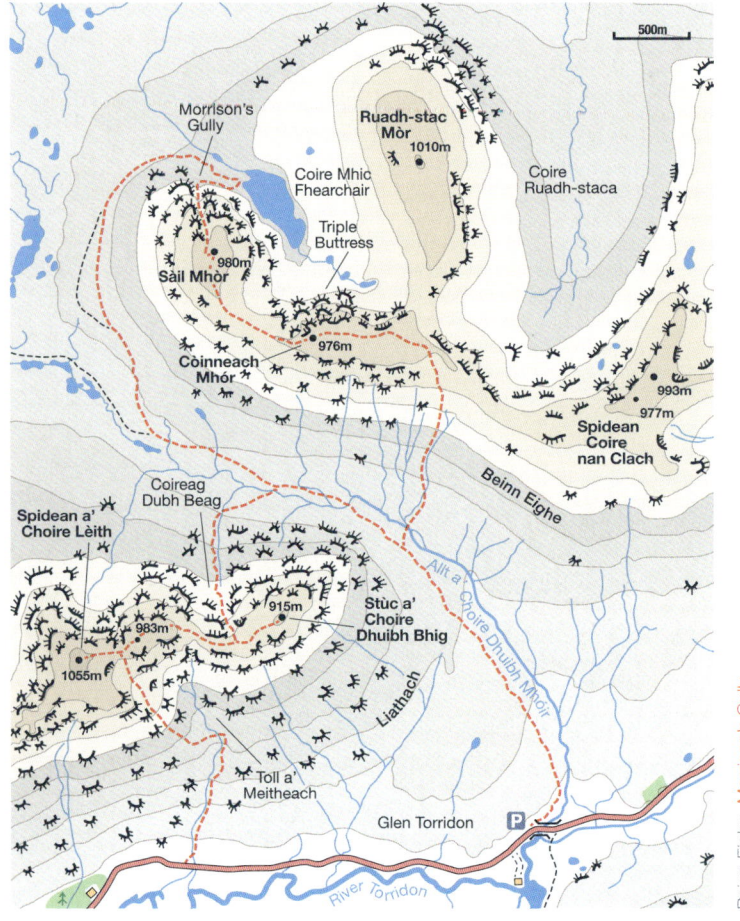

Beinn Eighe Morrison's Gully

Nearing the summit of Sail Mhòr overlooking the vast Torridonian hinterland - James and Adam Fisher

The huge cleft of Morrison's Gully splitting Sail Mhòr's north flank, seen from Beinn a' Chearcaill - Sheila van Lieshout

08 Liathach Main Ridge Traverse

Early season snow on Liathach's main ridge - Paul James

area
Torridon, Northwest Highlands

start
NG 935 566

difficulty
Grade II

distance
8.6km

total ascent
1410m

map
page 56

Probably the best ridge traverse on the mainland, on undoubtedly the finest mountain in Scotland A superb combination of high-level ridge walking and exposed scrambling surrounded by scenery of an otherworldly dimension. It is a magical winter journey in any conditions, even if there's just a dusting of snow.

The crux of the traverse is the crossing of the Am Fasarinen pinnacles, a series of narrow sandstone towers located midway between the mountain's two highest peaks. Following heavy snow, there may be no alternative to tackling the pinnacles other than by sticking to their crest. This can be a tricky and involved proposition. A winter traverse of Liathach may well be one of the most memorable mountain journeys of a lifetime.

Liathach Main Ridge Traverse

Background Liathach is located on the north side of Glen Torridon, approximately 8km west of Kinlochewe. Its seven distinct tops are spread along an imposing 5km-long ridge that runs in an east to west direction, parallel to the glen road. The mountain has two principal peaks, the higher being the pyramidal Spidean a' Choire Lèith (1054m), which sits in an almost central position on the ridge. Only marginally smaller, but of equal stature, is Mullach an Rathain (1023m), which overlooks Loch Torridon at the western end of the ridge. A broad shoulder pushes west beyond Mullach an Rathain, extending the mountain for a further 2km before dropping steeply to Coire Mhic Nòbuil.

Along most of the mountain's southern flank, steep terraced walls cascade down to the glen floor (at times from an unbroken height of nearly 1000m), conveying an overwhelming impression of impregnability. Towards both ends of the main ridge the terraced walls give way to a hanging corrie. These two high corries provide the easiest and most convenient means of access onto the ridge.

The northern side of Liathach, the 'far side', is a truly wild place. Here the mountain's flanks are carved into by a series of steep-sided corries, each with their own character. There is a wonderful charm and intriguing complexity to this side of the mountain, traits that can't really be appreciated by simply looking down from the ridge… best return sometime and do route 9.

Description Start 700m east of Glen Cottage on the A896 in Glen Torridon (NG 936 567). A small cairn marks the start of a path about 50m W of the stream, the Allt an Doire Ghairbh. The path crosses the stream then climbs steeply up its east bank into the bowl of Toll a' Meitheach. Continue up the east bank of the stream towards the rear of the corrie. If the line of the stream is buried under snow, head NNW up easy slopes, aiming for the dark, conspicuous gully that slices the corrie headwall. At 600m, contour right/E along a broad sloping terrace beneath the lowest significant rock band.

From the end of the terrace, adopt a rising rightward line across open snow slopes and through breaches in the occasional sandstone bluffs. A final easier-angled snow slope leads naturally to a col on the main ridge (833m). From the col a short detour E leads to Stùc a' Choire Dhuibh Bhig (913m), the easternmost peak on Liathach and a fine viewpoint.

Return W along the ridge and continue over the twin tops of Stob a' Choire Liath Mhòr (983m), before scrambling down into a prominent gap. A long, broad snow arête now leads up to the summit (1054m). In most conditions the going along this entire part of the ridge is straightforward. Expect continuous grade I terrain, both up and down. If the crest is covered with hard névé, well, just don't trip!

Approaching Mullach an Rathain. Early afternoon in mid-January and the sun already starting its descent over Loch Torridon - Steve Worth and Kath James

Liathach Main Ridge Traverse

From the summit of Spidean a' Choire Lèith descend SW, down an easy slope, to the small distinct notch that signifies the start of the Am Fasarinen Pinnacles. The pinnacles are usually tackled by a combination of their crest and some judicious shuffling along their left/southern flanks. Route finding isn't normally an issue, unless in very poor visibility when one or two spurs projecting into Coire na Caime can mistakenly be followed. A narrow summer traversing path, low down on the southern flank, is often steeply banked-out. Unless conditions are lean the path is best avoided.

Following on from the pinnacles is a long, gentle cliff-edge walk up to the summit of Mullach an Rathain (1023m). The views north across to Liathach's Northern Pinnacles and Meall Dearg are confusingly alpinesque. Whereas to the west, across Loch Torridon, and beyond to Skye and the Hebrides, the view can only be Scotland.

Return For the quickest descent (and the most convenient way back to the start), head initially W along a narrow projection, before bailing SE, down steep slopes, into the bowl of Toll Bán. A well-marked path leaves the bowl following the west bank of the steam, the Allt an Tuill Bhain. At 350m the path breaks from the stream and heads SSW. It then drops over numerous slabby sandstone terraces to meet with the Glen Torridon road at a small pinewood (NG 914 554), 1km east of the Torridon road junction. It is now a walk, or hitch, of just over 4km back to the start point.

If transport can be organised, a far more satisfying descent, especially if the sun still has some way to drop on a clear winter's day, is to continue W from Mullach an Rathain. A lovely 2.5km walk down uncomplicated terrain leads to the subsidiary peak of Sgòrr a' Chadail (678m). From here drop steeply NW to a flattening, from where a very rough path descends generally NNW, picking a way down through a series of steep sandstone bluffs. Cross open ground to meet with the Coire Mhic Nòbuil path, a short distance north of the Alligin car park (NG 869 576).

Liathach Main Ridge Traverse
Liathach North-South Crossing

Liathach Main Ridge Traverse

Finding a way across the Am Fasarinen Pinnacles. Helpful snow cover and no wind, but limited visibilty - Steve Worth

The steep and convoluted southern flanks of the Am Fasarinen Pinnacles, seen from the Glen Torridon road

09 Liathach North-South Crossing

The north side of Liathach. Stable weather following heavy snowfall in mid-March

area
Torridon, Northwest Highlands

start
NG 957 568

difficulty
Grade I

distance
8.4km

total ascent
1150m

maps
pages 52 & 56

To the 'far side' of Liathach and back again returning by an unlikely route over the mountain's highest peak, Spidean a' Choire Lèith (1054m). This is a technically easier and less committing undertaking compared to a main ridge traverse, but it certainly isn't 'Liathach light'. It is a completely different but equally good way of crossing the mountain in winter.

The crossing is at its most attractive if there is snow cover to below 650m or so. However, even in post-thaw or late season alpine conditions, when only Access Gully and Spidean a' Choire Léith's east ridge may be holding onto snow, it is still an exceptional outing. Despite being an intricate journey, navigation is never too difficult, with distinctive mountain features way-marking the whole route.

Liathach North-South Crossing

Background A mooch around any of Liathach's northern corries takes you into a truly ancient setting. The surreal outlook, across the primeval Torridonian hinterland, can suspend any rational, scientific explanation as to how the landscape was formed. Tucked away at the back of each corrie is a narrow snow gully. Each of these easy gullies leads directly onto the main ridge, allowing the possibility of a number of interesting ways to cross the mountain.

Running around the far side of Liathach is a well-made, 12km-long path. Starting from the east, it begins by climbing into Coire Dubh Mòr, the glen between Liathach and Beinn Eighe (there is a tendency for some glens to be called corries in Torridon), before continuing through to the wild and open setting at the head of Coire Mhic Nòbuil. The first of Liathach's northern corries seen from the path is the bowl of Coireag Dubh Beag. This is the smallest and most charming of the mountain's three main corries, whose unusual symmetry has a somewhat 'non-natural' quality.

The next corrie along is Coireag Dubh Mòr. It is slightly bigger and more open than its neighbour, and sits beneath the large, triangular cliffs of Spidean a' Choire Lèith. The most westerly corrie is the chaotic Coire na Caime, or *Crooked Corrie*, and is by far the largest and most spectacular of the three. It is encircled by alpine-like scenery, which together with its remoteness ensures that any visit has an atmosphere of backcountry exploration.

Description Start at the small car park on the A896 in Glen Torridon (NG 957 568), just W of the bridge crossing the Allt á Choire Dhuibh Mhoir. Follow the footpath up into Coire Dubh Mòr and around the east end of Liathach. After around 2.5km, a set of large stepping-stones allow the path to cross a wide stream. From roughly 300m beyond the stepping-stones, leave the path and strike SW across rough ground, towards the burn coming from Coireag Dubh Beag. A steep ascent on the west side of the burn leads up to the flat corrie floor.

The corrie is an almost perfect amphitheatre, enclosed by steep sandstone terraces that are often draped with ice smears. This really is a cool little corrie. Tucked back on the left are the entrance slopes to Access Gully, which climbs to a col on the main ridge (833m). The gully is 150m in length and keeps to the same gradient throughout. A problematic cornice would be rare. From the top of the gully a short detour E leads to Stùc á Choire Dhuibh Bhig (913m), the easternmost peak on Liathach and a fine viewpoint.

Return W along the ridge and continue over the twin tops of Stob a' Choire Liath Mhòr (983m), before scrambling down into a prominent gap. A long, broad snow arête now leads up to the summit of Spidean a' Choire Lèith (1054m). In most conditions the going along this entire part of the ridge is straightforward. Expect continuous grade I terrain, both up and down.

Looking back east along Liathach's main ridge, with surreal conditions in mid-February - Steve Cale

Liathach North-South Crossing

Return Head back down the E ridge of Spidean a' Choire Lèith, returning to the prominent gap at its base. From here, bail straight down a wide gully on the S side of the mountain. In favourable conditions this is a first-rate bum-slide, with a safe run-out onto a large flat area that is clearly shown on the map (NG 933 577). Continue directly across the flat area, aiming for a niche on its far side. The niche marks the top of another gully (narrower with rocky sides) that drops into the large open bowl of Toll á Meitheach.

Descend the entire length of this second gully and avoid tempting terraces branching out to the left that only lead to steep bluffs. From the bottom of the gully, contour left/E across the corrie floor to reach a well-made path on the far side of the stream, the Allt an Doire Ghairbh.

The path leads down to Glen Torridon and is easy to follow as it weaves through steep ground close to the east bank of the stream. It arrives at the road at a rough layby (NG 936 566), 700m east of the small Glen Cottage forestry plantation. It is now a walk, or hitch, of just over 2km back to the start point.

Heading towards Spidean a' Choire Lèith after climbing Access Gully.
High pressure in mid-february - Steve Cale, Andy Ollerton and Alexis Jones

Climbing up to Stùc a' Choire Dhuibh Bhig at the eastern end of the ridge - Alexis Jones

10 Beinn Alligin Deep South Gully

In the depths of Deep South Gully - Dave Lees

area
Torridon,
Northwest Highlands

start
NG 868 576

difficulty
Grade I

distance
10.4km

total ascent
1330m

map
page 64

A beautiful ridge traverse combined with a fantasy gully If journeys are about the places they take you along the way, then this journey takes some beating. It is incredibly varied, in both scenery and terrain.

Ascending Deep South is easy, except in lean conditions when there is often an icy squeeze beneath a chockstone, but this will only be of concern to tubsters. Good snow cover down to 400m is preferable, or at least it having snowed to this level in the preceding days. This increases the likelihood of the gully's boulder-covered floor being nicely filled-in. Crossing Beinn Alligin's Horns involves grade I scrambling, both up and down. It is more airy than exposed, but still easy to fall off.

Beinn Alligin Deep South Gully

Background Beinn Alligin is the most westerly of the three big Torridonian mountains and rises directly from the north shore of Upper Loch Torridon. It is a beautiful mountain, whose real aesthetic qualities can only be seen from its summit ridge. It is only from here that the elegant sweeps of the mountain's flanks and the natural symmetry of its peaks can be properly appreciated. The 3km-long, crescent-shaped ridge encloses a large east-facing corrie, Toll a' Mhadaidh Mòr. The wide corrie floor is strewn with boulders and rock debris, the result of a massive rock fall estimated to have happened nearly 4000 years ago.

There are two principal peaks on Beinn Alligin, both of which are Munros. Guarding the southwest end of the main ridge is Tom na Gruagaich (922m), whose summit plateau is incut by a high south-facing corrie, Coire nan Laogh. To the north, towards the centre of the ridge, is Beinn Alligin's highest peak, the classically shaped Sgùrr Mòr (986m). A prominent, steep-sided gash drops from just beneath its summit to almost the corrie floor. This is the Eag Dhubh, the huge scar remaining from the aforementioned rockslide.

The northeast end of Beinn Alligin's ridge is formed by the three narrow, rocky tops of Na Rathanan (866m), better known as the Horns of Alligin. Their steep northeast flank conceals one of the great gullies of Scotland, Deep South Gully, and a truly fantastic way in which to start a traverse of the mountain.

Description Start at a large car park adjacent to the bridge over the Abhainn Coire Mhic Nòbuil (NG 868 576), which is located 3km west of Torridon village on the single-track road to Inveralligin. From the car park, head NE along the east bank of the river, following a well-made path through lovely Caledonian woodland. After approximately 2km, cross the river at a footbridge, then continue N along the east bank of the subsidiary burn, the Allt a' Bhealaich. Ignore the better established Coire Mhic Nòbuil path, which branches off to the east.

Continue uphill for 800m to a footbridge and cross to the west side of the burn. The path then continues climbing N for a further 500m before arriving at a junction. Take the right fork and continue N, towards the Bealach a' Chòmhla; the pass between Beinn Alligin and Beinn Dearg. The exact route of this path is difficult to follow under snow, but it takes a logical line staying approximately 200m uphill of the burn.

The beautiful symmetry of the southeast face of Sgùrr Mòr, seen from the Horns of Alligin

Beinn Alligin Deep South Gully

Continue towards the bealach until directly beneath the first gully on the northeast-facing cliffs of the Horns. This is Deep South Gully. Ascend the snow apron and enter its depths (NG 879 610). The main part of the gully is chasm-like, hemmed in on either side by huge walls. Near its top, the gully constricts and curves to the right. At this point it is sometimes necessary to squeeze through a gap beneath a stack of jammed boulders. When buried they create a short, easy step. The gully exit is always steep but never harder than grade I. It emerges at the col between the first (easternmost) and second horn.

From the col, scramble NW over sandstone tiers to the turret-like summit of the second horn. An easy descent into the col beyond is followed by a further short scramble onto the third and highest horn (866m). The elongated top forms a narrow level ridge. The short walk to its far end is something special; with an ocean outlook directly ahead and Sgùrr Mòr's beautiful southeast face dominating the view to the left.

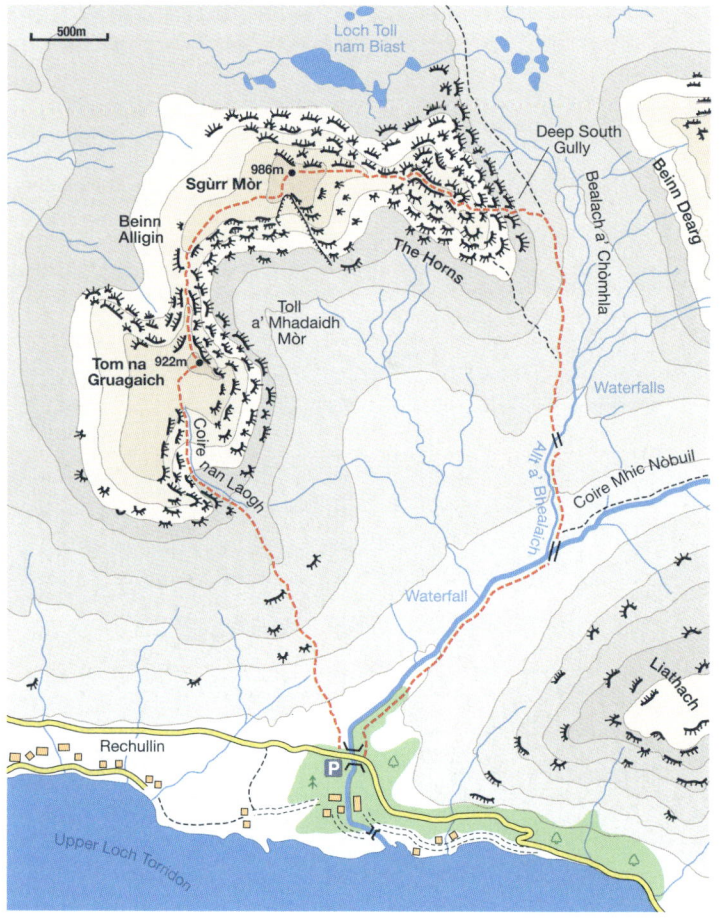

Beinn Alligin Deep South Gully

From the small cairn at the end of the ridge, descend SW, down steep snow and through broken rock bands, before veering WNW to reach the col at the base of Sgùrr Mòr's long east ridge. An easy walk up the broad crest leads directly to the summit (986m). Occasional backward glances during the ascent reveal ever-expanding views of the Torridonian hinterland.

In poor weather, leave the summit bearing W to avoid the cliffs at the head of the Eag Dhubh, *the Black Cleft*, before veering SW at 940m. Otherwise, head S and don't miss the opportunity to visit this unusual mountain feature. Continue easily around the rim of the corrie, crossing a minor top (cairned) before reaching the flat col (767m) at the base of Tom na Gruagaich's pronounced north ridge.

Head up the ridge, with some easy scrambling and one very short, exposed section near its top. The actual summit is elevated above the summit plateau and is a grand end-of-day viewpoint. It would not be difficult or stressful to descend safely from here in fading light.

Return From the trig point head SW, which leads directly into the catchment trough at the head of Coire nan Laogh. In favourable snow conditions it is possible to bum-slide almost the entire length of the corrie. A rough but easy to follow path leaves the bottom of the corrie and takes a more-or-less direct line back to the car park.

The summit plateau of Tom na Gruagaich and the expanse of the Torridonian mountains - Dave Lees

11 Beinn Damh The Traverse

On the east-southeast spur of Beinn Damh, with the mountains of the Coulin Forest as a backdrop - James Whitmore

area
Torridon, Northwest Highlands

start
NG 889 541

difficulty
Grade I

distance
11.4km

total ascent
1080m

map
page 68

An easy peak with an 'out there' feeling Stunning situations combined with little technical difficulty; this is a mountain journey that tips a toe into Scottish winter mountaineering. It is best reserved for a day with a good chance of some clear weather.

Being a coastal mountain, Beinn Damh may not have the sustained snow cover of its inland neighbours, nevertheless it is frequently in a satisfactory wintry condition. A snowline of 600m or below will give a continuous winter traverse of all the mountain's five tops. A higher snowline, along with cold weather, still opens the door to a good winter outing, as is often the case during easterly winds.

Beinn Damh The Traverse

Background Beinn Damh is located some 5km southwest from the mouth of Glen Torridon. It is a grand mountain in many ways. However, it is the wonderful connection with both the sea and the inland mountains, created by a 4km-long summit ridge, that makes it special. The northern end of the ridge looks directly over Loch Torridon and has seascape views far beyond to the Minch and the Atlantic. Whilst at the southern end of the ridge, the mountain's summit, Spidean Coire an Laoigh (903m), stands in splendid isolation on the fringes of the rough mountainous expanse of the Coulin Forest.

A winter traverse of Beinn Damh is best undertaken from south to north, gaining the summit via its short east-southeast spur, the Stuc Coire an Laoigh. The spur is secluded and feels un-frequented. It is also a far easier proposition than its initial appearance would suggest; the steep flanks seen on the approach are misleading and give no indication of the spur's broad, easy-angled crest.

In essence, climbing the Stuc Coire an Laoigh is all about a feeling of space and remoteness, which it manages to give out in abundance. Its ascent is actually an integral part of traversing Beinn Damh; turning a good winter hill walk into an exceptional but still easy mountaineering journey.

Description Start by the Loch Torridon Hotel on the A896, 2km west of the road junction leading to Torridon village (NG 889 541). There are parking spaces on the verges close to the bridge over the Allt Coire Roill, just beyond the hotel. A good stalker's path leaves the road 100m W of the bridge and heads S through the stumps of a cleared rhododendron thicket. It then climbs up through native Caledonian pine, all the time staying well above a deep river gorge. At the head of the gorge is an impressive 30m waterfall, which is easily visited with a slight detour from the path.

Just beyond the waterfall, as the woodland thins out, the path divides. Take the left fork and head SE to a ford that crosses the Allt Coire Roill. On the east bank of the river go briefly downstream for 50m before turning sharply right and following a well-made path that heads SE towards the top of the glen. After 2.5km the path skirts the south shore of a small lochan just before reaching a broad col, Drochaid Coire Roill. The col overlooks a long, open glen, the Srath á Bhàthaich, beyond which is the mountainous interior of the Coulin Forest

From the col head SW up a very broad rib, climbing a number of small, steep sandstone tiers by the most direct line as possible. The rib eventually leads onto a small mound, Meall Dubh na Drochaid (581m), from where Beinn Damh's Southeast Spur, the Stuc Coire an Laoigh, can be seen in its entirety. Contour around the bowl of Coire an Laoigh, passing beneath the cliffs on its far side, to gain the base of the spur.

Beinn Damh's east-southeast spur, the Stuc Coire an Laoigh - Graham Burns and Storm Bates

Beinn Damh The Traverse

The lower part of the spur is just steep enough to warrant grade I and can be enlivened by staying to the right and scrambling up turfy grooves. At no point is it ever exposed and easier ground can always be gained by simply moving left. At 780m the angle eases off to straightforward walking terrain. Continue up the spur as it curves up to Spidean Coire an Laoigh (903m), Beinn Damh's isolated summit.

Return Head WNW down a well-defined ridge to reach a slender col. Now head NW over a minor top, then on to a second more prominent, unnamed top (868m). From here, bail N down a fine ridge, which leads into the bowl of Toll Bàn. Cross the corrie floor in a NW direction to reach the summer descent path on the far side of the Allt an Tuill Bhàin. Follow the eroded path NE down to a junction with the approach track, just above the waterfall. Stroll happily through the woodland back to the road.

If visibility is good and time allows, it is well worth visiting Sgurr na Bana-Mhoraire (687m), the prominent peak at the northern end of Beinn Damh (think magical sunset). To do this, descend NW from the unnamed top (868m), down a broad ridge, to reach a long, flat saddle. Continue NW over the subsidiary top of Meall Gorm (675m), then climb steeply up to the trig point and an outstanding viewpoint. For the easiest, or in fading light, least complicated descent, retrace your steps SE to the saddle, then drop NE on the eroded summer path as previously described.

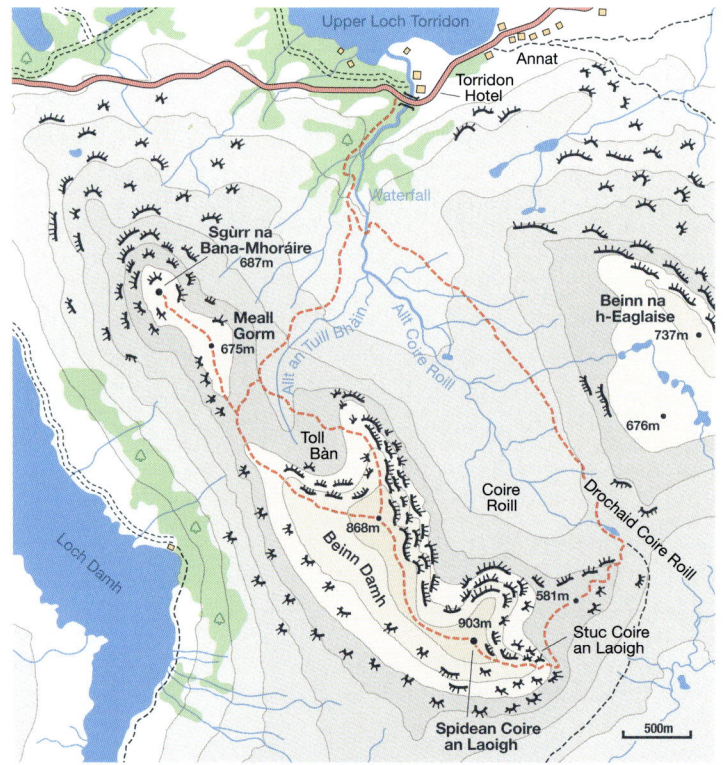

12 Beinn Bhàn A' Chìoch Traverse

Reaching Beinn Bhàn's summit plateau in fading light, after a traverse of A' Chìoch in early January - Paul James

area
Applecross, Northwest Highlands

start
NG 835 422

difficulty
Grade II

distance
10.2km

total ascent
1050m

map
page 72

Superb mountaineering on an utterly compelling line The traverse of the narrow crest of A' Chìoch and the subsequent climb onto Beinn Bhàn's summit plateau is absorbing from start to finish. It is a journey starting in deep, unearthly corries and whose high point is an open summit with expansive views across to Skye and the Hebrides.

The upper connecting ridge is steep and committing, and at times very exposed. With consolidated snow it offers excellent winter scrambling, at a difficulty that is pretty much what you'd expect for the grade. However, in lean conditions, or under powder, the ridge becomes quite hard; careful route finding is required to sniff out the easiest line. All climbing sections are sheltered from westerly winds and the entire route is safe from avalanche.

Beinn Bhàn A' Chìoch Traverse

Background Beinn Bhàn (896m) is the highest and most imposing of the Applecross Hills, a small group of mountains located on the landward side of the Applecross Peninsula. They are close to the sea but are often in a wintry condition, surprisingly often in fact. Especially when it comes to being good enough for winter mountaineering. Although isolated, the range is easily accessed from the A896, the old west-coast road connecting Loch Carron and Loch Torridon.

The 8km-long summit ridge of Beinn Bhàn runs in a northwest to southeast direction. Towards its centre it is just wide enough, and flat enough, to be considered a plateau. The whole northeast side of the mountain is a fascinating place, formed by a series of six corries. Two of these, Coire na Feola and Coire na Poite, are particularly funky, with deep and intriguing layouts. Each rises from an outer corrie to a hidden inner corrie that is enclosed by magnificently high, terraced walls.

Coire na Feola and Coire na Poite are separated by a narrow steep-sided ridge, whose outer end supports a great castellated tower, A' Chìoch. At its inner end, where it connects with the main mountain, the ridge steepens abruptly, shooting up in an unbroken line, straight to the summit plateau. The quality of any mountaineering line is measured as much by its situation as by the standard of the actual climbing, the traverse of A' Chìoch excels in both these criteria. Judge for yourself.

Description Start at a small layby (NG 835 422) on the causeway over the Kishorn estuary, at the head of Loch Kishorn. This is on the road to Applecross, 450m beyond the junction with the A896 at Tornapress. Cross the road bridge and head N along a good track for approximately 2km. At a footbridge over the Allt Coire na Feòla, stay on the south side of the stream and head W up a faint path, towards the mouth of Coire na Feòla. It is possible to cut uphill towards the corrie sooner but rough, heathery ground does not make this direct line much quicker.

From the flattening just inside the corrie, strike N and zig-zag up onto the lower shoulder of A Chìoch. Now head easily up the broad crest to reach a small plateau at the top of the first tower (730m). From here, the panoramic spectacle of Beinn Bhan's eastern cliffs is awesome.

Continue towards Beinn Bhàn, initially down a block-covered ridge then onto concave snow slopes. At the end of the slopes, climb down a steep groove to reach the small col at the base of the second tower. Either climb directly up the second tower, or by a depression just to the left of its crest. The top of the tower is spanned by a narrow snowy arête (716m). From the far end of the arête, descend steep snow on the right/N, before curving back left along a ledge to reach the slender col at the base of the upper connecting ridge.

The top of A' Chìoch's first tower, on a guided traverse with visiting American climber Glenn Zhann

Steep and exposed shizzling on the upper connecting ridge of A' Chioch - Paul James

Beinn Bhàn A' Chìoch Traverse

The gully on the left/S side of the col can be descended into Coire na Feòla (grade I) and still makes for a good, short mountaineering day. It is an option to have in the back pocket, especially if topping out in extremely strong westerlies might be an issue. The upper ridge can be climbed by a number of possible ways, generally keeping within a short distance of the crest. Steep turfy grooves, exposed snow slopes and some tricky walls can all be expected. The line of least resistance is described below.

Pick a way up the centre of the ridge until stopped by a steep wall at around 50m. The breach in the wall would once have had plenty of turf; it is now bare rock. With a build-up of snow, climbing the groove is not a problem. In lean conditions, it's a bit of a bugger. An easier but more exposed alternative is found to the right.

Easier ground quickly leads to a second rock barrier. This is climbed via a distinctive v-shaped chimney. A chockstone thread can provide security. Without helpful snow, a direct line up the final steepening can feel quite insecure. Instead, take a rising leftward line over large blocks, then cut back right and ascend easier-angled slopes to reach the top of the difficulties. A narrow arête then leads to the summit plateau. Beinn Bhàn's summit lies 400m to the NW.

Return Strike SE from the summit trig point, retracing your steps to the plateau area. Continue down the long SE ridge, being aware that cornices are likely around the rim of Coire na Feòla. Cross a minor top (763m) and then continue descending to where the ridge loses definition (670m). From here veer ESE, down an open and uncomplicated hillside, directly back to the Kishorn estuary causeway.

13 Sgorr Ruadh Academy Ridge & Post Box Gully

Gaining the summit of Sgorr Ruadh, in the middle of the wild landscape of the Coulin Forrest - Sheila van Lieshout

area
Glen Carron,
Northwest Highlands

start
NH 005 483

difficulty
Grade II

distance
13.4km

total ascent
1030m

map
page 79

A there and back again journey, to a wild Northwest peak The ascent of this extraordinary Scottish mountain follows a long but beautiful approach walk, through the heart of an unfrequented winter landscape.

From a distance, the upper section of Academy Ridge looks improbably steep. However, just as the ridge becomes too difficult, the line of ascent sneaks rightwards into a hidden narrow gully, Post Box Gully, which provides a superb grade II snow climb to the summit plateau. Despite being well-constructed, the approach path, like any other mountain trail, has the potential to become arduous after heavy snowfall. In these conditions, climbing Post Box Gully is also likely to be questionable.

Sgorr Ruadh Academy Ridge & Post Box Gully

Background Sgorr Ruadh (962m) is the highest peak within the rough mountainous country that separates Glen Carron and Glen Torridon. This wild tract of land is historically known as the Coulin Forest, a term used to denote an old hunting ground rather than woodland. It is a mishmash of unusually shaped mountains separated by long, wide-open corries, creating the jumbled landscape that is unique to this part of Scotland. A network of excellent stalkers' paths threads through the forest, making a journey to its interior manageable within a short winter's day, and nothing like the schlep it might otherwise be.

Sgorr Ruadh sits at the head of Coire Láir, in a roughly central position in the Coulin Forest. From the lip of the corrie the view is dominated by the mountain's extensive and convoluted northeast facing cliffs. These cliffs give the mountain a squat, fortified appearance, particularly as they are unchallenged by the flat expanse of the surrounding corrie floor. Perched at the top of the cliffs, and hidden from view, is a small plateau area. At its western end the plateau gives way to gentle snow slopes, which gradually rise by 100m to a pronounced summit cone. This tiny summit, in the middle of nowhere, is the destination of this journey.

Description Start at Achnashellach on the A980 (NH 005 483), 500m northeast of Loch Dughaill in Glen Carron. There are parking spaces near to the station access track, on the opposite side of the road to the phone box. Follow the track to the station and cross the line at the platform. Head NE up a forestry track for 100m, then turn sharp left at a junction. Continue along the track for 600m until a cairn and a small sign, which mark the start of a narrow path leading down towards the river.

Just beyond a deer fence the path joins what used to be the original route into Coire Láir, which, from this point onwards, has been re-built to a very high standard. Follow the path as it climbs steadily out of the woodland and weaves its way up through small sandstone bluffs and past isolated stands of Caledonian pine. At round 360m the terrain opens out into Coire Láir and Sgorr Ruadh comes into view. Continue NW along the path towards the head of Coir Láir, ignoring two turn-offs; the first going west towards Bealach Mòr and the second heading northeast towards the col at Drochaid Coir Láir.

Sgorr Ruadh from the Coire Láir path. Academy Ridge beneath the shadow, rising leftwards at 45 degrees - Sheila van Lieshout

Sgorr Ruadh Academy Ridge & Post Box Gully

The exit slopes to Post Box Gully, which lead straight onto the summit plateau of Sgorr Ruadh - Sheila van Lieshout

Icy conditions low down in the excellent and hidden Post Box Gully - Sheila van Lieshout

Sgorr Ruadh Academy Ridge & Post Box Gully

Even though the line of Academy Ridge is easily identified from any point on the path, the best place to scope the layout of Sgorr Ruadh's cliffs is from a few hundred metres beyond Loch Coire Láir. From this location, the mountain's furthest skyline is the outline of the steep Raeburn's Buttress. Coming left of this, and dividing the cliffs, is the wide hollow of Central Couloir. Bounding the left side of the Couloir, and partially obscuring it, is Academy Ridge, which is broad and easy-angled in its lower part and steep in its upper section. Left of this are the Southeast Cliffs, a kilometre-wide broken area cut by three long rakes, running up from left to right.

Leave the path and cross the Allt Coire Láir, which is usually possible from anywhere upstream of Loch Coire Láir. Once across, take a direct line towards the toe of Academy Ridge. The ridge is climbed by weaving up through a series of sandstone tiers via a choice of corners and grooves (difficult under powder or unconsolidated snow). Failing this, skulk around to the right, into the beginnings of Central Couloir, and gain the crest of the ridge at the first amenable opportunity.

Walk up the crest of the ridge, effectively a broad shoulder, to where it steepens abruptly. Now traverse right, along a sloping shelf, to where it is possible to drop a few metres into a hidden narrow gully, Post Box Gully (the gully's origins are way below this point, in Central Couloir). Head up the exquisite gully, which may have three short icy steps, depending on build-up. A problematic cornice would be unusual. The gully's exit slopes pop out onto the eastern end of a small undulating plateau. Strike W across the plateau, skirting the top of Central Couloir before climbing gentle snow slopes that lead up to Sgorr Ruadh's remote summit cone.

Return Descend E from the summit, retracing your steps as far as the top of Central Coloir. Bail down the atmospheric couloir, which, if you're lucky, is one of the top bum-slides of the Northwest. From the bottom of the couloir, head back across the corrie floor and regain the approach path on the far side of the Allt Coire Láir... and so to Achnashellach.

Approaching the summit cone of Sgorr Ruadh on a windy mid-February day, with visiting Dutch climber Mark Willem

14 Fuar Tholl The Crossing

Nearing the summit of Fuar Tholl on a harsh January day - Paul James and Matt Hawkins

area
Glen Carron,
Northwest Highlands

start
NH 005 483

difficulty
Grade I

distance
9km

total ascent
905m

map
page 79

A good, honest winter journey Fuar Tholl is an attractive mountain with an unusual layout. It is close to the road yet has an air of neglect. This winter crossing weaves its way through the mountain's southeast and northwest corries, giving a journey that is low in difficulty but a scenic treat. A brief section of exposed ridge enlivens the way up.

The ascent is objectively safe in any snow conditions. This also goes for the way down if a variation is taken via the mountain's northwest ridge. A major drawback occurs when the River Làir is in spate, as fording anywhere downstream of Coir Làir becomes impossible. In which case, a rethink is required and Fuar Tholl may have to wait for another day.

Fuar Tholl **The Crossing**

Background Fuar Tholl rises up at the head of Strathcarron, on the southern edge of the Coulin Forest, the rough mountainous country that separates Glen Carron and Glen Torridon. The mountain's southern slopes are featureless and uninteresting. From all other aspects the topography is touching on captivating, with an ad hoc arrangement of tilted buttresses and steep sandstone cliffs. One buttress in particular, the massive Mainreachan Buttress, which juts incongruously from the side of the northwest ridge, is a magnificent piece of rock. To stand dwarfed beneath it is reason alone for traversing the mountain.

The southeast corrie of Fuar Tholl is nestled just below the summit and clearly visible from the road at Achnashellach. Throughout the winter an almost permanent snowfield covers the long slopes leading up to the corrie headwall. The snow seems resilient to even the harshest thaws, perhaps accounting for the mountain's name, meaning *Cold Hole*. There is a much grander feel within this corrie than its small size would suggest. The frequent presence of huge cornices above the headwall adds to this impression.

Fuar Tholl's northwest corrie, Coire Mainnrichean, is open and wild, with an outlook reaching far across the Coulin interior. Easy-angled slopes at the rear of the corrie provide an uncomplicated way down the mountain. An excellent stalker's path then connects with the main Coire Láir path, which in turn meanders pleasantly down to Achnashellach. A cruisy finish to what will already have been a top winter day.

Description Start at Achnashellach on the A980 (NH 005 483), 500m northeast of Loch Dùghaill in Glen Carron. There are roadside parking spaces opposite the station access track, near to the phone box. Follow the track to the station and cross the line at the platform. Head NE up a forestry track for 100m, then turn left at a junction. Continue along the track for 600m until a cairn and a small sign, which mark the start of a narrow path leading down to the river. Ford the river by an old weir and climb S onto the brow of the hill, the southeast shoulder of Sgùrr á Mhuilinn.

It would obviously be quicker and easier to reach the same point by walking a short distance W along the railway track from Achnashellach station and then crossing the bridge. This would save fording the river (which is dangerous if in spate). However tempting this may be, it is an offence to trespass on the railway line.

A faint and intermittent track runs from the railway line, up the length of the broad shoulder of Sgùrr á Mhuilinn. Pick up the path and pass through a gate in the deer fencing that spans the hillside at the 200m contour. From the flattening at 400m, aim for the stream flowing from Fuar Tholl's southeast corrie and ascend rough ground on its east side. The area around the small lochan at the bottom of the corrie is sheltered from all but southerly winds.

Fuar Tholl from the east, with the curving profile of the southeast ridge dropping to the left in the foreground

Fuar Tholl The Crossing

From the lochan, ascend N over rocky terraces to reach a small col at 640m. Beyond the col are Fuar Tholl's north facing cliffs, which drop steeply into Coire Làir. Head W up easy ground to the beginnings of the wee southeast ridge. At first the ridge is broad and straightforward. It is only for a short final section that it becomes quite narrow, with appreciable drops on either side. Then bang, it's over, and the summit plateau is reached. The summit shelter is 200m to the SW. In poor visibility be aware of the likelihood of large cornices on the left, extending a surprising distance over the corrie rim.

Return Head SW from the summit shelter, down gentle slopes, to a wide col at 860m. From here, bail NW down steep slopes into Coire Mainnrichean. If snow conditions are favourable, this, along with Central Couloir on Sgorr Ruadh, is one of the top bum-slides of the Northwest. World-class in fact. Continue descending NW to pick up the Bealach Mòr path 200m beyond the corrie's small lochan.

In suspect snow conditions, or to simply stay up high longer, head W from the col, across the top of the Mainreachan Buttress (895m). Beyond the buttress, veer NW over a small rise (857m), before dropping steeply through a band of crags. The crags are more broken and easier to descend to the true-left/W. From the base of the crags, head N to pick up the Bealach Mòr path, 200m beyond an elongated lochan.

The path is well-constructed but its line is not easy to follow under deep snow. It meanders for just over 2km across rough ground, in a general NE direction, to arrive at a fording point across the River Làir (NG 989 502). There are no better crossing places downstream. Cross the river and follow the excellent Coire Làir path SE, as it weaves down through sandstone bluffs and alpinesque scenery to meet with forestry tracks used on the approach… and so to Achnashellach.

Fuar Tholl The Crossing
Sgorr Ruadh Academy Ridge & Post Box Gully

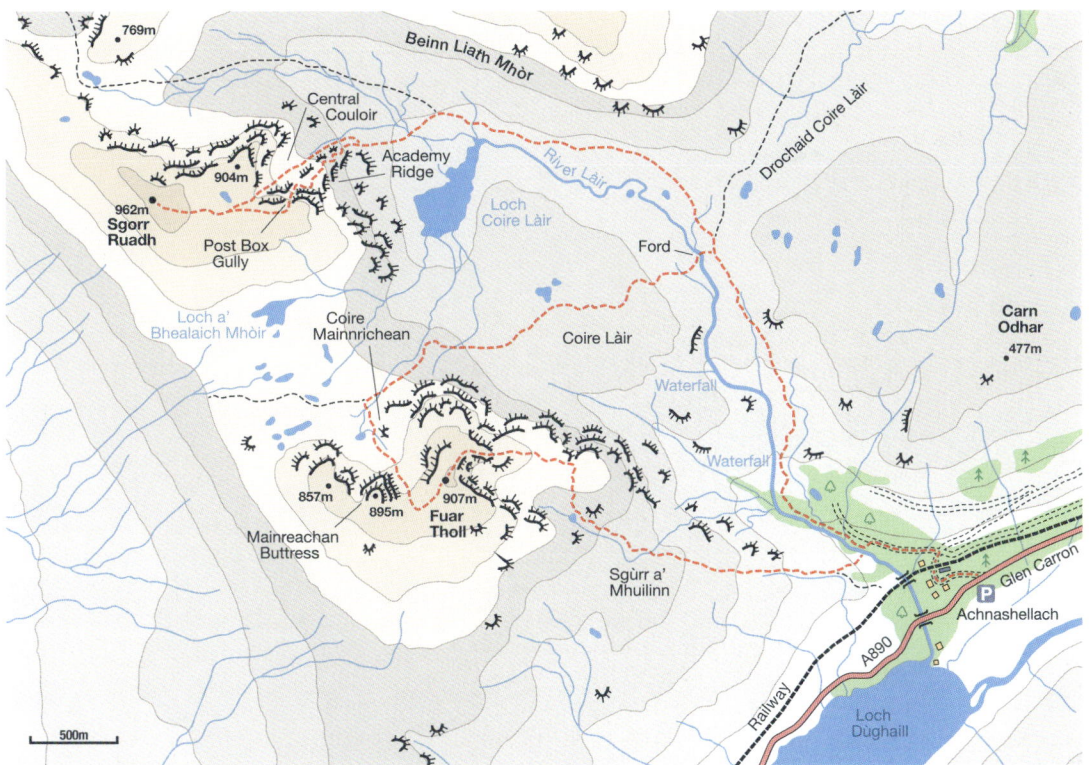

15 Sgùrr nan Gillean The Traverse

The Southeast Ridge of Sgùrr nan Gillean, with Pinnacle Ridge in the background - Robin Thomas

area
The Cuillin, Skye

start
NG 484 297

difficulty
Grade II

distance
11.6km

total ascent
1060m

map
page 82

As good as it gets The traverse of this classically shaped peak on the Isle of Skye is completely captivating, involving a tricky and exposed ridge on both the way up and the way down. All the time surrounded by incomparable views across the sea to the Hebridean islands and the mainland mountains.

Although the approach to the base of the southeast ridge is straightforward in clear weather, it can be very confusing in poor visibility. The actual traverse is a committing undertaking without any escape options and requires a good repertoire of mountaineering skills. There is an obligatory 20m abseil on the descent.

Sgùrr nan Gillean The Traverse

Background The Cuillin of Skye is a narrow 12km-long ridge of some 35 rocky peaks, rising straight from the sea. And it's located on one of the most beautiful islands in the world. On a clear day, the Cuillin's unmistakable, jagged outline is visible from many of the mainland's west coast ranges. Always enticing, always calling. Mountaineering on Skye is special at any time of year, being the perfect combination of mountains, sea and sky. In winter it takes on an additional dimension and should be sampled at least once in a lifetime

With Skye's position on the edge of the Gulf Stream, the Cuillin don't have the consistency of snow cover that is common on many mainland hills. However, it is a myth that good winter mountaineering conditions on Skye are rare. Snow falls often; it just doesn't stay around for very long or build-up to any extent. As such, planning a winter trip to Skye in advance isn't wise. The best tactic is to keep an eye on weather and conditions. And when they show promise, pounce.

Sgùrr nan Gillean sits at the northern end of the Cuillin ridge, above Sligachan. It is a superb mountain from all aspects, with three fine ridges converging at a sharp summit to create its distinctive triangular profile. A traverse of the mountain by two of these ridges, up the southeast and down the west, gives an outing not dissimilar in feel to an alpine climb… and the best single axe journey on the island.

Description Start at a layby next to the mountain rescue building on the A863 (NG 484 297), 200m SW of the Sligachan Hotel. Head SSW along a well-made footpath across the open moor. After 300m cross the Allt Dearg Mòr on a newly constructed footbridge and continue SSW along an equally good path. At a fork, take the left branch, over a footbridge crossing the Allt Dearg Beag, and follow the subsequent path that climbs slowly S to the brow of a broad shoulder. The path then descends a little before contouring S across the hillside into the floor of upper Coire Riabhach.

At the far side of Coire Riabhach, a scruffy path picks its way up a steep scree slope onto the top of a rise. Beyond the rise is a large open slope, scree at first but then strewn with boulders. Head S across this rough ground (cairned), then at its far side veer SW to be funnelled into a small, narrow corrie that is unnamed on OS maps (NG 477 254). Break through a rock barrier, the corrie headwall, by a slanting leftward line, to reach another large open slope, which is the northern flank of Sgùrr nan Gillean's southeast ridge. Zig-zag up this to reach the crest of the ridge and a panorama of the whole Cuillin cirque.

The obligatory abseil down the steep Nicolson's Chimney on the descent of the west ridge - Robin Thomas

Sgùrr nan Gillean The Traverse

Climbing the left-hand rake near the top of Sgùrr nan Gillean's southeast ridge - Robin Thomas

Sgùrr nan Gillean The Traverse

Just to reiterate, the route to this point would be confusing in poor visibility. And finding a way across the large boulder field beyond Coire Riabhach would be extremely time consuming under deep snow. Worth a punt though, if there's a chance of being on the ridge and the weather clearing.

It's also worth mentioning that the southeast ridge is more commonly known as the Tourist Route. A misleading name that was likely only intended to indicate the easiest route up the mountain and not meant to infer that it is easy, which it isn't.

Head directly up the ridge, which is straightforward at first being mainly walking with the occasional short scrambly step. After a few hundred metres the ridge narrows and steepens markedly. Continue on the crest until a broad rake materialises on the left/south side of the ridge. With helpful snow it's possible to continue directly up the crest, otherwise veer left and take an easier line into the rake. As the rake steepens, ascend a distinctive shallow groove. At its top, cut back right and move across terraces for a short distance to the base of a steep corner. A series of three short, spicy steps leads back onto the crest of the ridge.

The final section of ridge is very narrow and almost horizontal. It is exposed but not difficult. Only one short, awkward gap bars access to the summit. Step boldly across this to reach the small summit blocks and one of the world's great mountain views.

Return Scramble down the W ridge, taking a line that alternates between the crest and a few metres below on the right/N flank. At a tower cross to the left/S side of the ridge and pass through a window or, if this is blocked by snow, climb over the top of the tower. A short distance beyond the window, a featureless and almost slabby section of the ridge may require an abseil, depending on snow cover. There is an ideally positioned spike for the 12m abseil.

Continue more easily down the ridge until the way ahead is blocked by ground that suddenly, and obviously, becomes far too difficult. At this point, on the right/N side of the ridge there is a steep chimney, Nicolson's Chimney. A 20m abseil will kiss the ledge at the base of the chimney (large block anchor, not always with in situ gear). Follow the ledge W to rejoin the crest of the ridge beneath the difficult ground. Continue easily along the crest, now the headwall of Coire a' Bhàsteir, to its lowest point, Bealach a' Bhàsteir.

From the bealach, drop N down easy snow slopes towards the small lochan in Coire a' Bhàsteir. The route from the corrie to the moors south of Sligachan is well trodden and marked by cairns, but is complicated enough to need care if obscured by snow. From 150m downstream of the outlet, contour N across slabby ground (passing beneath a distinctive cave - a useful landmark), staying well above the west side of the gorge. When the ground begins to drop, veer slightly to the NNW, away from the gorge, and pick a way down through steep slabby steps. From the base of the slabby rock band, a short scree or snow slope leads easily down to the moorland.

On the moorland, pick up a well-established path that sticks to the west bank of the Allt Dearg Beag. After approximately 2km, the path veers off to the NNE, directly towards Sligachan. This is now the same path used on the approach.

Approaching Bealach a' Bhàsteir with the imposing Am Bàsteir dominating the way ahead - Robin Thomas

16 Bruach na Frithe via Sgùrr a' Bhàsteir

On the lower slopes of the northeast ridge of Sgùrr a' Bhàsteir, facing the Pinnacle Ridge of Sgùrr nan Gillean - Ian Hey

area
The Cuillin, Skye

start
NG 484 297

difficulty
Grade I/II

distance
12.6km

total ascent
1005m

map
page 82

A mountain journey of dreams A wonderfully varied route that winds its way through a fairytale landscape. A landscape that offers far more than just an aesthetic appeal. If this place doesn't lift your spirit, nowhere will.

The route can be attempted in all snow conditions. In limited visibility, it is still an excellent, atmospheric outing that is never too tricky to navigate considering the complexity of the terrain and the reputation of the Cuillin. Essentially, this is winter mountaineering on Skye, at a very amenable grade.

Bruach na Frithe via Sgùrr a' Bhàsteir

Background Bruach na Frithe (958m) is one of the easiest peaks in the Cuillin to climb. But this is not to its detriment; it is a beautiful mountain that just happens to be surrounded by more difficult and imposing peaks. Its summit has arguably the finest viewpoint on the ridge, providing an unbroken panorama across the entire range, which goes some way in explaining the choice of location for the Cuillin's only trig point.

Along with Sgùrr nan Gillean (see route 15), Bruach na Frithe is located at the northern end of the Cuillin, above Sligachan. When winter arrives on Skye, this is where snow cover will likely linger the longest, particularly in the high north-facing corries of Coire a' Bhàstier and Fionn Choire. Logistically, this is also the most accessible part of the Cuillin, being less than 40 minutes drive time from Kyle of Lochalsh. With an alpine start, and some determination, it can be reached from as far afield as Fort William or Inverness, arriving at a still sensible time to walk-in (there's accommodation on the island too!).

By approaching Bruach na Frithe over the neighbouring peak of Sgùrr a' Bhàsteir, and descending by the mountain's long northwest ridge, a winter journey is created that just about stays within the category of grade I. Only briefly, on the descent, does the difficulty of the terrain edge above this. Despite the route choice managing to keep the difficulty low, there is no attempt at avoiding exposed terrain, an impossible job in the Cuillin.

Description Start at a layby next to the mountain rescue building on the A863 (NG 484 297), 200m SW of the Sligachan Hotel. Head SSW along a well-made footpath across the open moor. After 300m cross the Allt Dearg Mòr on a newly constructed footbridge and continue SSW along an equally good path. After 1.5km the path hits the Allt Dearg Beag, from where it continues along the west bank of the stream towards the Bhàsteir Gorge; the deep ravine emanating from Coire a' Bhàsteir

Approximately 400m before the gorge, the path veers away from the stream and heads S, towards the crags to the right of the gorge. Head up the apron slopes beneath the crags, either on snow or well-trodden scree, and begin picking a way through the slabby ground above. The cairned access path to Coire a' Bhàsteir starts contouring S at around 520m, staying well above the gorge. Follow this rough path for around 100m, then at the first amenable opportunity break SW, steeply uphill.

The climb from the Coire a' Bhàsteir path to the summit of Sgùrr a' Bhàsteir (898m) is an ascent of close to 400m. The going is rough at first but is more than offset by a gradually unfolding backdrop of the spectacular Pinnacle Ridge of Sgùrr nan Gillean (964m). As height is gained, the broad slopes merge to form Sgùrr a' Bhàsteir's northeast ridge. From around the 700m contour the ridge becomes well defined and a narrow crest leads easily up to the small and dramatically positioned summit.

Sgùrr a' Bhàsteir on the left and Bruach na Frithe on the right. Seen from the head of Glen Brittle

Bruach na Frithe via Sgùrr a' Bhàsteir

Sgùrr a' Bhàsteir is connected to the main Cuillin peaks by a narrow and more-or-less horizontal ridge. Head S along this 450m-long ridge, which in all likelihood will be a snow arête. Across the corrie to the left is the perfectly formed pyramid of Sgùrr nan Gillean. Right of this is the unmistakable jagged outline of Am Bàsteir (934m). Directly ahead is the narrow col of Bealach nan Lice, which provides a passage through to the remote Lota Corrie in the heart of the Cuillin. Right again, is the steep, squat face of Sgùrr a' Fionn Choire (930m), and over to the far right, across Fionn Choire, is the beautifully shaped Bruach na Frithe. This is exceptional mountain scenery.

At the far end of the ridge, pinch yourself before traversing right/W, to contour across easy snow slopes beneath the north face of Sgùrr a' Fionn Choire. Beyond the face, take a rising line to gain the crest of the main ridge, which is then followed without difficulty to the trig point on Bruach na Frithe's airy summit.

Return From the trig point, head directly down the defined crest of the NW ridge. After dropping 120m or so, the ridge steepens abruptly, necessitating a brief, tricky diversion onto the left/W flank. At this point, climb down steep rocky ground on the left, being wary in poor snow conditions of the uniform slopes lower down on the flank. After descending 50m or so, contour NW along ledges to regain the crest beneath its steepening. Continue down the ridge without any further difficulty.

Lower down, the northwest ridge gradually loses its definition. Continue across open ground towards Bealach a' Mhàim (344m), the highest point on the path connecting Glen Brittle and Sligachan. Pick up this excellent path on the far side of some small lochans and head NE alongside the Allt Dearg Mór, back towards Sligachan.

High on the crest of Sgùrr a' Bhàsteir's northeast ridge, with a snow-capped Red Cuillin behind - Ian Hey

Easy going on the main Cuillin ridge between Sgùrr a' Fionn Choire and Bruach na Frìthe - Ian Hey

Bruach na Frithe via Sgùrr a' Bhàsteir

Reaching the main Cuillin ridge after crossing Sgùrr a' Bhàsteir's summit ridge - Ian Hey

Descending Bruach na Frithe's long northwest ridge, with the Hebrides on the distant horizon - Ian Hey

17 The Saddle Forcan Ridge

The upper section of the Forcan Ridge on an atmospheric day in early January - Toby Keep

area
Glen Shiel,
Northwest Highlands

start
NG 967 144

difficulty
Grade I/II

distance
9.9km

total ascent
1110m

map
page 95

A classic mountaineering route with the feel of an alpine ridge Long, wonderfully airy and engaging from start to finish. Its position, high above Glen Shiel, gives far-reaching views over a sea of peaks.

Climbing the ridge is feasible in all conditions. It is arguably better with heaps of snow but it is still good with any level of cover. A series of attractive snow arêtes often form along the upper section, beyond Sgùrr na Forcan. The higher element of the grade reflects an ascent sticking to the ridge's crest, which is frequently the only option.

The Saddle Forcan Ridge

Background A long chain of peaks stretches along the entire southern side of Glen Shiel. At its eastern end, starting above Loch Cluanie, the chain takes the ordered form of one continuous, undulating ridgeline known as the South Glen Shiel Ridge. Towards its western end, near Loch Duich, this single ridgeline loses its identity and is replaced by a more complex arrangement of ridges and scattered peaks, centred around the glen's most striking mountain, the Saddle (1010m).

The Saddle is situated approximately 6km south of Shiel Bridge, directly across the glen from the Five Sisters of Kintail. The outline of the Saddle, along with that of its neighbour Faochag (909m), dominates the view from the valley when travelling west towards the coast. Their appearance is fairytale; they are shaped how mountains are imagined, impressively tall and piercingly sharp.

Although the ridges above Glen Shiel are generally narrow, and in some cases quite steep, the majority fall just short of requiring a mountaineering approach. An exception to this is on the east side of the Saddle, where a striking knife-edge ridge climbs up to the satellite peak of Sgùrr na Forcan, before connecting, in a final dramatic sweep, with the mountain's east summit. This is the Forcan Ridge, a rite of passage for those who love Scottish winter ridges.

Description Start in Glen Shiel, at a layby on the A87 (NG 967 144), ½km southeast of the roadside quarry at Achnagart. A further 200m up the glen, on the S side of the road, is the start of a stalker's path. The well-constructed path heads SSW across open ground. It then zig-zags up a broad shoulder before taking a rising traverse across the northeast face of Meallan Odhar (610m). The flat col at the top of the rise gives the first unobstructed view of the Forcan Ridge.

From the col, head SSW along a narrow path, which traverses across the northwest flank of Meallan Odhar towards the wide saddle at the base of the ridge. The path is difficult to see under deep snow, in which case going over Meallan Odhar may be just as quick.

A rocky groove leads onto the broad crest of the ridge, which is followed without difficulty onto a minor top. From here on, the ridge narrows. Airy walking at first is followed by short easy sections of scrambling as the ridge climbs slowly towards Sgùrr na Forcan (963m). Brilliant.

Looking back along the Forcan Ridge towards Glen Shiel. Late March and sub-zero temperatures in the shade

Clearing mist for the final push on the Forcan Ridge - Toby Keep

The Saddle Forcan Ridge

Easy ground on the central section of the
Forcan Ridge - Toby Keep and Martyn Eade

Crossing Meallan Odhar towards the base of the
Forcan Ridge - Toby Keep and Martyn Eade

A short distance beyond the top of Sgùrr na Forcan, the direct continuation along the crest involves a steep descent. This is best abseiled. Without super-helpful snow, down-climbing either flank, as per the summer route, is going to be sketchy. The abseil is steep enough to warrant taking a harness and is just possible with a 30m rope (normally an in situ thread anchor).

The remainder of the ridge is neither difficult nor overly exposed. Exquisite snow arêtes are frequently the case on this final 500m stretch, and seem to form with just the hint of wind. A short scramble up to a subsidiary top (958m) is followed by a long sweeping dip, which rises steeply up at its far end to the east summit of the Saddle (1010m). The true summit (1010m + a little bit) is located 200m to the SW, along a straightforward connecting ridge.

Return From the trig point on the true summit, head S for 250m (descending to the 920m contour), then veer ESE, towards Bealach Coire Mhàlagain. This avoids convex slopes immediately to the southeast of the summit, which can often be suspect. Just before reaching the bealach, head NE and contour beneath the Forcan Ridge, back towards its base. A useful navigational aid is to follow an old section of wall, which traverses the hillside at 720m.

From the wide saddle at the base of the ridge, retrace the approach route across the northwest flank of Meallan Odhar, back towards the head of the stalker's path. A quicker alternative, when there is favourable snow cover, is to head E from the saddle, taking a line across the southeast flank of Meallan Odhar. On the far side of the hill, plunge-step or bum-slide down steep but easy slopes to intersect with the stalker's path... and so to Glen Shiel.

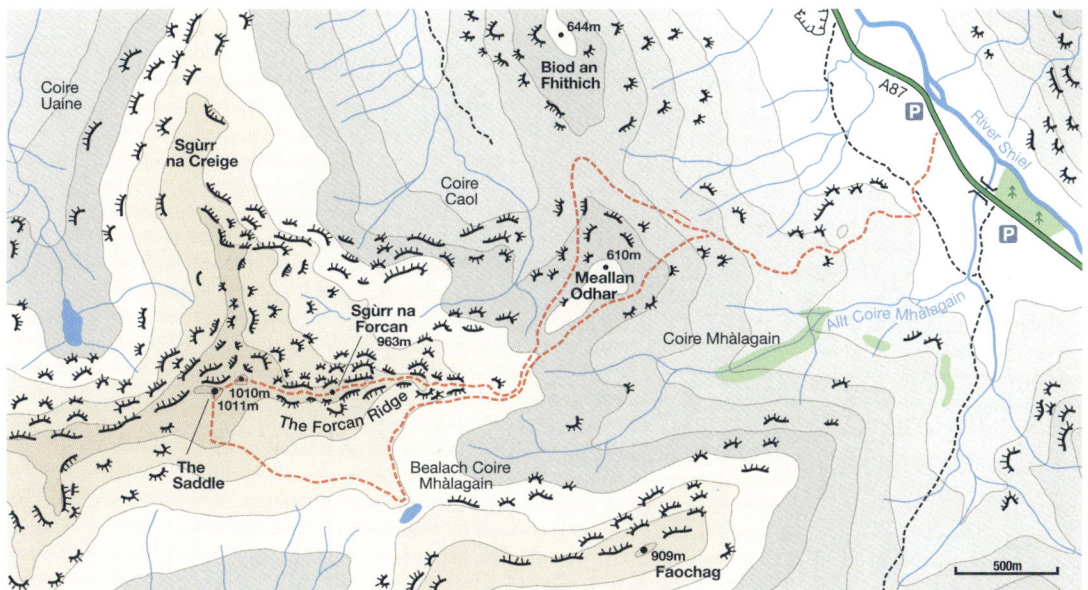

18 Aonach air Chrith North Ridge

The rock pinnacles on the crest of Aonach air Chrith's wee north ridge - Sheila van Lieshout

area
Glen Shiel,
Northwest Highlands

start
NH 051 114

difficulty
Grade I

distance
9.4km

total ascent
995m

map
page 98

A wee gem of a ridge Short yet surprisingly eventful. When combined with an ascent of the nearby Maol Chinn-dearg, it creates a delightful circuit with a lofty mix of easy winter scrambling and high-level ridge walking. Being entirely above 900m, it is frequently in a good wintry condition.

This ridge should never be thought of as just a 'plan B', but it is well worth considering as a last minute back-up. If conditions are poor in the more popular areas around Glencoe and Ben Nevis, its location, at the head of Glen Shiel, is surprisingly quick to reach from Fort William.

Aonach air Chrith North Ridge

Background The South Glen Sheil Ridge lies at the eastern end of Glen Shiel and has nine prominent peaks, including seven Munros, scattered along its 14km length. The ridge's crest is continuously narrow but never exposed. Only once does it drop below 800m. Its northern flanks, clearly visible from the A87, are a succession of deeply recessed corries interspersed by long subsidiary spurs that project towards the road. Conversely, the entire southern side of the ridge comprises one long, uniform slope dropping down to the remote Easter Glen Quioch.

In winter the South Glen Sheil Ridge is ridge walking heaven. There is the ability to go from peak to peak, along uncomplicated, easy-going ridges, all the while staying up high amongst stunning mountain scenery. Owing to its length, the ridge is most commonly enjoyed in segments, with easy access onto and off the crest using the subsidiary spurs. Given the right snow conditions, and good hill fitness, a single push traverse is a classic expedition.

The highest peak on the ridge is the shapely Aonach air Chrith (1021m), whose short, pronounced north ridge is virtually hidden from the road. This little ridge breaks the South Glen Shiel mould; its sharp rocky crest and steep flanks nudging it into the realms of mountaineering territory. It is a lovely way in which to gain the main ridge and is, in fact, more than good enough to be an objective in its own right.

Description Start in Glen Shiel, at a large crescent-shaped layby on the north side of the A87 (NH 051 114), 2.5km west of the Cluanie Inn. Head S across open ground, aiming towards the northern slopes of Aonach air Chrith. There is a vague, intermittent track but it is hardly worth seeking out; the terrain is neither as rough nor as boggy as it appears from the road. Unless in spate, the feeder streams into the River Cluanie are all easy to cross.

As the gradient increases, veer SSE up easy slopes, aiming for the small bowl-shaped corrie nestled beneath the shoulder of A Chioch (831m); Coire na Doire Duibhe (but un-named on the 1:50,000 map). From the corrie lip, head SW and pick a way up the broad spur bounding the west side of the corrie. The spur quickly becomes more defined and rises steeply before merging with the shoulder of A Chioch, to form the beginnings of Aonach air Chrith's north ridge.

Head along the ridge - this is narrow and airy, but never quite crosses the threshold of becoming 'properly exposed'. It is however, possible to fall off without much effort. Pleasant scrambling over a few minor rocky tops leads to a brief knife-edge section. An easy snow slope then climbs up to Aonach air Chrith's small summit dome.

A break in the squally snow showers crossing Aonach air Chrith and the only visibility of the day - Sheila van Leishout

Aonach air Chrith North Ridge

Return For a short day, go back down the north ridge and retrace the approach route to the valley. The ridge is just as good in reverse and doing it again compensates for its brevity. There's also the change of outlook, with the expansive views across the glen to the huge bulk of the Sisters of Kintail giving the ridge a bigger feeling than on the way up. The steep descent back to Coire na Doire Duibhe can be remarkably fast in the right snow conditions.

For the complete circuit, descend SW from the summit cairn and stroll across the long, sweeping ridge that connects to Maol Chinn-dearg (981m). Head NE from the summit dome, down gentle slopes for 400m, to the top of a pronounced spur. Descending this is steep at first but easy, and quickly eases-off onto a long broad shoulder. At the far end of the shoulder, a well-constructed stalker's path zig-zags down to the valley, arriving at the road 700m west of the start point.

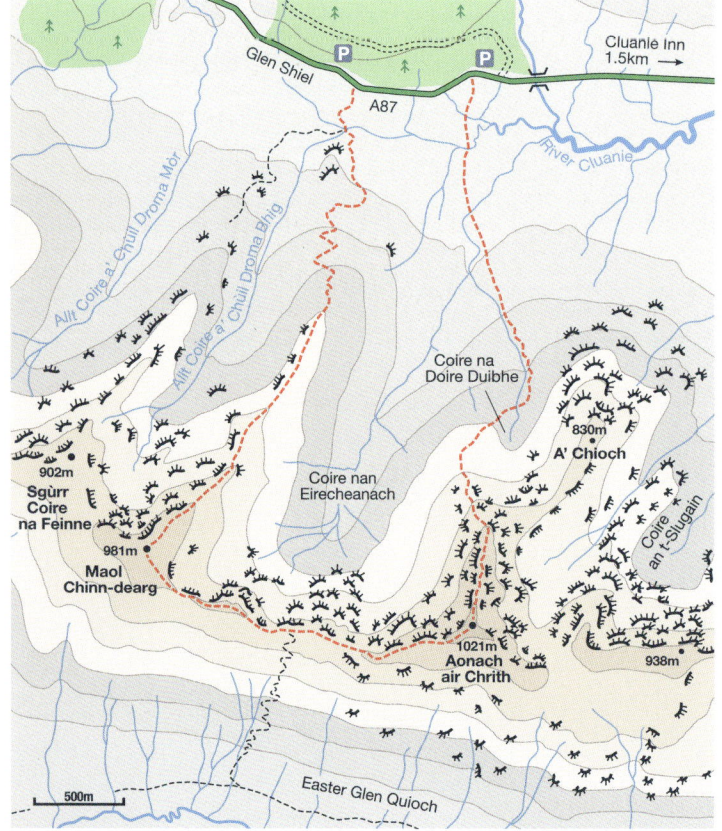

19 Beinn a' Chaorainn East Ridge

Scrambling on the upper crest of the East Ridge on a cold January day - Sophie Holdstock

area
Glen Spean, Central Highlands

start
NN 400 818

difficulty
Grade I

distance
9.7km

total ascent
805m

map
page 101

A good mountaineering outing on a surprisingly fine line especially considering the rolling appearance of the mountains within which it hides. With careful route choice the ridge can be a safe objective in virtually any snow conditions, even immediately following heavy snowfall. Both the ridge and the approach are completely sheltered from westerly winds.

Large accumulations of snow are a common and attractive feature on the upper part of the ridge. However, in lean conditions the route unfortunately loses some appeal. The exception to this is following a hard freeze, when steep turf can still give a good day of enjoyable winter scrambling. Crossing the summit plateau requires care in poor visibility; otherwise the descent route is uncomplicated.

Beinn a' Chaorainn East Ridge

Background Beinn a' Chaorainn is situated on the northern side of Glen Spean, approximately 30km east of Fort William. Along with its neighbour Beinn Teallach, it forms the western end of a stretch of mountains often referred to as the Laggan Hills. The uninspiring appearance from the Glen Spean road is misleading; long uniform slopes and a lack of any proud summit suggest a 'lump' of a mountain that offers little in the way of mountaineering interest.

It is only when glimpsed from a short section of the A86 near Moy Lodge, during a break in the dense, roadside forestry plantations, that the true nature of the mountain is revealed. It is here the crags of Coire na h-Uamha come briefly into view. These tall, sweeping cliffs extend along the entire length of the mountain's east flank and are an impressive sight in winter, especially when capped with their usual grand array of cornices.

Three distinct spurs punctuate the Coire na h-Uamha crags. The most northerly spur, furthest from the road and almost completely obscured by forestry, is by far the most striking. This is Beinn a' Chaorainn's East Ridge and the mountain's gift to those who love Scottish winter ridges.

Description Start 3km east of the Laggan dam on the A86 (NN 400 818), at the stone bridge crossing the river flowing from Coire na h-Uamha (parking places 30 metres east of the bridge). Head up a rough path on the east side of the river, the Allt na h-Uamha. Wooden stakes mark the way. After 450 metres the path reaches a recently constructed metal road bridge (NN 401 823). Cross the bridge and continue N along the edge of the forestry plantation as far as a deer fence. Now head W, between the fence and the plantation, to meet with a maintained forestry track (see notes on page 156 regarding ongoing tree harvesting and an alternative approach to this point).

Head N on the forestry track and follow it into another plantation. After approximately 2km the track emerges at the plantation's northern edge (the current OS map fails to show the full length of the track). At the tree line, turn W and head across open moorland to reach the toe of the East Ridge. Easy slopes lead onto a broad shoulder.

Head up the start of the ridge without any difficulty. The first steep section is ascended on the right/N, before veering back left/S to reach the base of a rocky barrier. Climb up through the barrier using a short couloir on the left, which from below appears as a niche on the skyline. At the top of the couloir is a second rocky barrier. Climb this direct (steep), or scoot around to the right/N and ascend a short rightward-leaning ramp, before cutting back sharply to the left/S onto the crest of the ridge.

Approaching the East Ridge of Beinn a' Chaorainn on a bright December morning - Dave Lees

From now on, stick to the crest wherever possible. In very snowy conditions, take care crossing the head of a narrow, north-facing gully (coming up from the right), located a short distance before the top of the ridge. In poor visibility the final 75m-long snow slope can be a hugely disorientating place; it is uniformly angled at 15 degrees, featureless and is where the effects of any howling westerly will first be felt. Striking directly uphill on this final slope will put you on a safe collision course with the small summit cairn, a short distance onto the plateau.

Throughout the winter season, monumentally sized cornices are a constant feature along the eastern edge of the plateau. In places, the potential fracture lines of these cornices extend far enough into the plateau to prevent a direct walking line to the mountain's south summit. Avoiding them is simple but can be a steely navigational exercise in a whiteout!

The south summit is a surprisingly good viewpoint, giving an unusual aspect on some familiar peaks. The chain of the Grey Corries is seen in its entirety, as are the eastern flanks of Aonach Mòr and Aonach Beag. Peeping above these is the summit of Ben Nevis.

Return The easiest descent is to head S, down straightforward slopes to approximately the 600m contour. Now veer SE and sidle into the wide gap between Point 628m and Meall Bhàideanach (606m). From the gap, head in a general E direction as far as a plantation fence line. Follow this downhill to meet with the maintained forestry track used on the approach. Head S down the track and retrace the approach route back to the A86 Glen Spean Road.

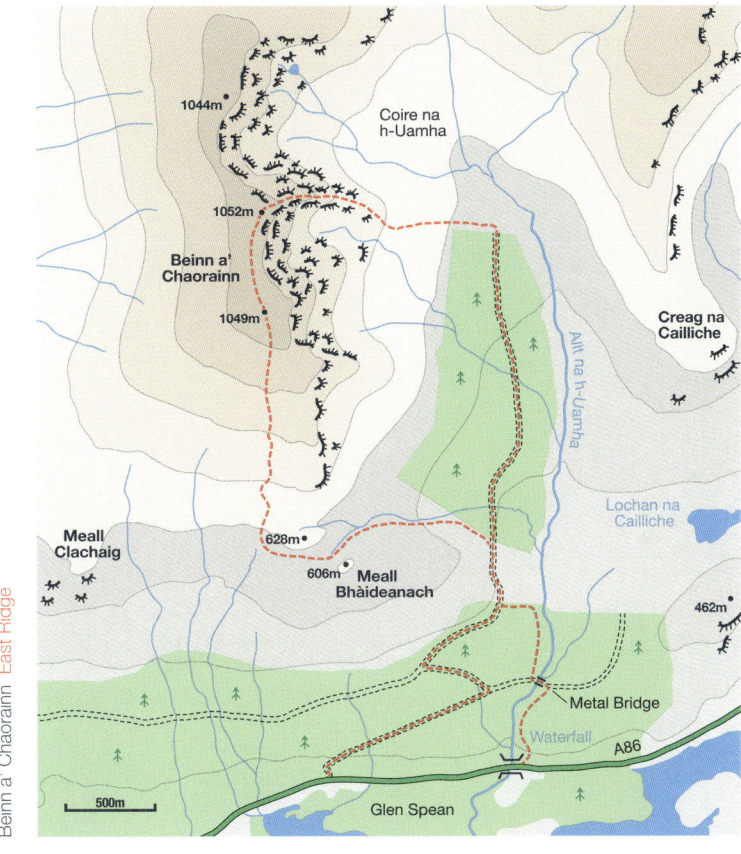

20 Creag Meagaidh Raeburn's Gully

Approaching the cliffs of Coire Ardair - Sheila van Lieshout

area
Glen Spean,
Central Highlands

start
NN 483 873

difficulty
Grade I

distance
15.6km

total ascent
960m

map
page 104

An easy gully climb that oozes big mountain ambience Set within the grandeur of the Coire Ardair cliffs, Raeburn's Gully sneaks up the side of the soaring 450m-high Pinnacle Buttress; a place where it feels a grade I gully shouldn't go. The gully faces north but owing to the corrie's unusual layout and the adjacent high plateau, it collects snow from unexpected directions.

Recent woodland regeneration and a much-improved Coire Ardair path make for a pleasant and often easy-going approach walk. In poor weather, navigating across the summit plateau is notoriously confusing. There are a number of attractive return routes.

Creag Meagaidh Raeburn's Gully

Background Creag Meagaidh is to the north of Glen Spean, just above the southern tip of Loch Laggan, approximately 35km east of Fort William. It is a large, sprawling mountain with a flat and featureless summit plateau at its centre. Several broad ridges radiate outwards from the plateau, enclosing a number of deep corries between them, the most impressive of which is the northeast-facing Coire Ardair. This long, curving corrie is home to an extensive array of high cliffs and buttresses that have come to define Creag Meagaidh.

Despite Coire Ardair's low elevation, its cliffs are rarely without a wintry appearance. The rolling summit topography causes westerly storms to pour huge amounts of snow over the tops of the buttresses, building large cornices and creating deep accumulations in almost every recess and hollow throughout the corrie. When Creag Meagaidh has been blootered, it is one of the great sights of the Highlands. And well worth catching when bathed in early morning light.

Creag Meagaidh is better known for ice climbing than for mountaineering, with the steep runnels of the Post Face and the drainage lines in the Inner Corrie providing heavenly ice when 'in condition'. But these great cliffs aren't solely about technical climbing. A few easy mountaineering circuits do exist, allowing you to be very much within the mountain and to soak up the 'Meggie' atmosphere. Any mountaineering journey on Creag Meagaidh should always begin with a walk up Coire Ardair and an ascent of Raeburn's Gully.

Description Start at the Creag Meagaidh Nature Reserve car park at Aberarder (NN 483 873), halfway along Loch Laggan on the A86. Follow the footpath NW towards the farmhouse, now a National Nature Reserve (NNR) centre. Continue on a well-made path that starts on the right of the building and winds uphill on the north side of the Allt Coire Ardair. The path stays well above the stream and passes through an extensive area of young birch woodland, the result of an ongoing NNR regeneration programme. The older, broken trees scattered on the hillside at the far end of the woodland are the result of large avalanches that have swept across the path. As the glen curves to the west, the Coire Ardair cliffs slowly come into view.

The path eventually descends towards the floor of the glen, then runs alongside the stream, as far as the Lochan a' Choire. The lochan's outlet is as good a spot as any to get familiar with the layout of the corrie. The first buttress to the left is Bellevue Buttress, which is separated from the nearby towering Pinnacle Buttress by the long leftward-leaning line of Raeburn's Gully. To the right of Pinnacle Buttress is Easy Gully, above which rises the huge Post Face, identified by its four steep runnels or Posts, often ice-choked in their lower reaches.

An atmospheric descent through Coill a' Choire, the birch woodland of Coire Ardair - Sheila van Lieshout

Creag Meagaidh Raeburn's Gully

To the right of the Post Face the cliffs curve away beyond a huge prow, Great Buttress, into the elevated Inner Corrie. The intricate nooks and crannies of the Inner Corrie's cliffs are obscured from view. The cliffs terminate at the Window, the prominent bealach that lies between the main bulk of Craig Meagaidh and the satellite peak of Stob Poite Coire Ardair (1054m) on the right.

Cross the outlet of the lochan and skirt around its southern edge before breaking SW, up easy slopes towards the wide entrance to Raeburn's Gully. The gully is steeper than it appears from the corrie floor, and sustained. The exit is steeper still, but only for 40m or so and 'not quite' grade II. Any cornice can usually be passed on the right. During extended cold periods a chandelier of blue ice often forms on the Pinnacle Buttress wall, two-thirds of the way up the gully. On occasions it can create an enclosed windbreak big enough to accommodate two people.

Return In a case like this it is hard to recommend a return route. In such big open country the choice is inevitably going to be dictated by visibility… and, as always, how far you'd like to walk.

Given reasonable visibility, skirting across the plateau to descend via the Window will give the most intimate experience of Coire Ardair's cliffs and is described as follows. From the top of Raeburn's, head NW for 250m to reach the southern tip of the Post Face cliffs and the top of Easy Gully (itself an optional atmospheric descent into the corrie). Continue in a NW direction across the plateau towards the Window. After 1km the plateau begins to drop markedly, at this point veer WNW to avoid the line of bluffs forming the southern edge of the Window.

Craig Meagaidh Raeburn's Gully

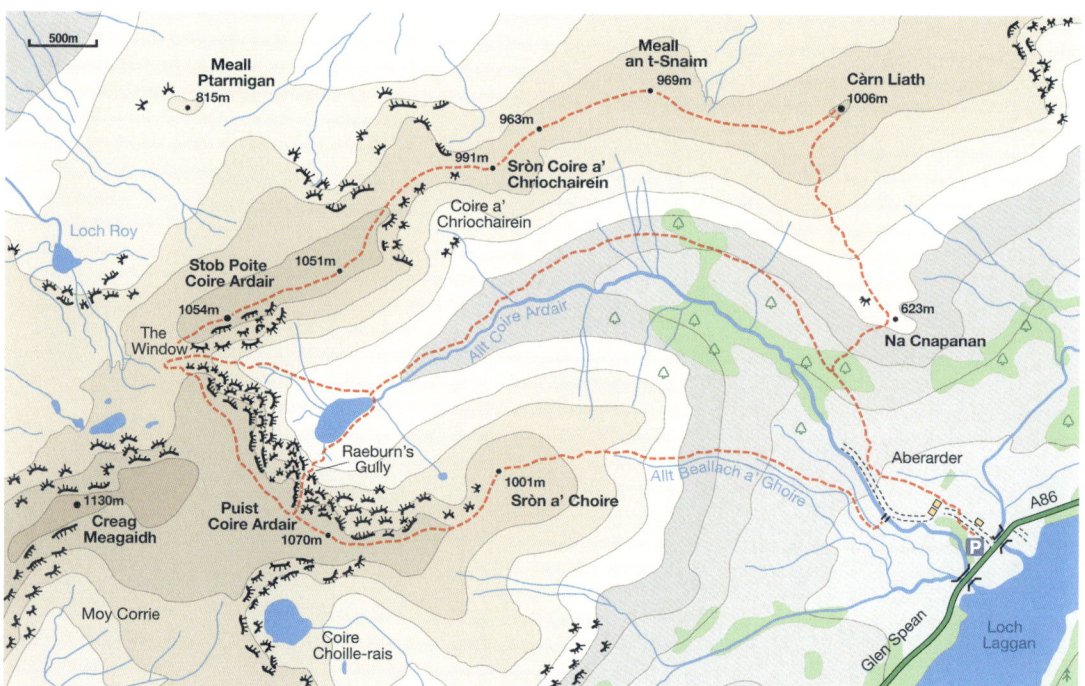

The towering Pinnacle Buttress with Raeburn's Gully running up the left-hand side

It's worth stating again that crossing the featureless plateau in poor visibility can be a very disorientating exercise, despite essentially being a straight-line walk. Trust an old-school compass and bearing approach, and be conscious that the plateau has subtle changes of aspect deliberately designed to confuse. The tops of the Coire Ardair cliffs switch between being concave and convex in shape, or are corniced, so will be useless as a navigational handrail. At the far side of the plateau reassurance is provided by a spaced line of old fence posts that lead down to the Window.

The Window is a weird feature, almost like a sunken small valley or dell. It collects huge volumes of snow and it would be unusual for there not to be elaborate shelters dug into its deep snow banks; it is a popular location for spending a night out in a snow hole. Descend E from the Window, down easy slopes that pass directly beneath the buttresses and gullies of the Inner Corrie. From the lochan follow the Coire Ardair path back to Aberarder.

A return can also be made along the broad ridges on either side of Coire Ardair, staying high above the glen. The quickest way back to Aberarder, and the easiest to navigate in crappy weather, is via the ridge of Sròn a' Choire (1001m) on the south side of the glen. From the top of Raeburn's Gully, head SE over the indistinct top of Puist Coire Ardair (1071m). Then head E, following the cliff edge around to the summit dome of Sròn a' Choire (there is a line of old metal fence posts set 25m back from the edge). Descend ENE from the summit, into a wide shallow corrie. The easiest ground is likely to be found by staying north of the Allt Bealach a' Ghoire in the lower part of the corrie. There is a footbridge across the main river 300m west of the NNR centre.

The ridge on the north side of the glen gives the longest return route and is the way to go for a big walk on a fine weather day. The uncomplicated rolling terrain presents no difficulties; it is a pleasant, high-level winter ramble. Climb steeply N from the Window then veer NE onto the broad top of Stob Poite Coire Ardair (1053m), the first of two Munros on this ridgeline. Continue E over a subsidiary top and skirt around the rim of Coire a' Chriochairein. From the top of Sron Coire a' Chriochairein (991m), at the far side of the corrie, drop NE into a peculiar trench-like notch.

Climb out of the notch and continue ENE for 1km to reach the indistinct summit of Meall an t-Snaim (969m). Descend ESE to a col and then start the long gradual ascent to the almost flat summit of Càrn Liath (1006m), the second Munro on the ridgeline. From the large summit cairn, head SW and follow the broad shoulder that curves down to the SE, onto Na Cnapanan (623m); the small spur sitting above Aberarder. A vague track leads WSW to meet with the Coire Ardair path.

21 Càrn Dearg Meadhonach East Ridge

The summit tower of Càrn Dearg Meadhonach. The northeast buttress of Ben Nevis in the distance - Steve Worth

area
Fort William, West Highlands

start
NN 171 774

difficulty
Grade I

distance
9.7km

total ascent
850m

map
page 111

A funky little ridge overlooking a bleak winter landscape It is an unexpected and attractive mountaineering line in an otherwise desolate looking glen. Granite blocks that cover the crest ensure a fun ascent whatever the conditions. The top of the ridge provides big time views across the north face of Ben Nevis.

Despite the ridge's remote setting, the nearby Nevis Range ski area provides a relatively short approach. It is a safe route in all snow conditions (so long as a sensible line is taken when dropping into the Allt Daim glen from the ski area following easterly winds). Deep snow would make gaining the base of the ridge arduous.

Càrn Dearg Meadhonach East Ridge

Background Càrn Mòr Dearg (1221m) is a long, slender mountain that lies between Ben Nevis (1344m) and Aonach Mòr (1221m) and stretches in a north to south direction. The southern tail of the mountain's spine curves round to form the Càrn Mòr Dearg arête (route 22), by which it is joined to Ben Nevis. There are three tops to Càrn Mòr Dearg, the middle of which is Càrn Dearg Meadhonach (1179m), *the Middle Red Cairn*, notable for its short but pronounced east ridge. The crest of this ridge supports three blunt towers and is littered with huge granite blocks. It is ideal for winter scrambling.

The ridge drops towards the Allt Daim, a bleak and barren glen that would be a bit of a haul to access if it weren't for the convenience of the nearby Nevis Range gondola. The uplift provided by the gondola, to 650m, opens this whole area to quick-hit mountain journeys that would otherwise only be undertaken by the Billy Whizzes of this world. These gondola-assisted journeys are only possible on the proviso of fair weather (the gondola doesn't run in strong winds), and when mixed with the good café facilities of the ski area, make for strangely civilised Euro-type outings.

Càrn Mòr Dearg's main summit is also blessed with an attractive east ridge, located at the head of the Allt Daim. This easy-angled ridge runs down to meet a high windy col at right angles, giving it the propensity to form into a lovely snow arête. It provides a nigh on perfect, stress free descent route from the mountain.

Description Start at the Nevis Range ski area beneath Aonach Mòr (NN 171 774). The access road to the ski area is located 7km northeast of Fort William, at a well-signposted turn-off on the A82. The gondola runs for a 10 minute window, starting at 8am, every day throughout the winter, a service specifically for climbers and hill walkers. With the gondola being affected by strong winds, the service is sometimes suspended in adverse weather. The status of the service can be checked by phoning the ski area (+44 (0)1397 705 825) or by keeping an eye on social media updates on the Nevis Range accounts.

From the top gondola station turn right and head WSW, along a wide track that contours across the ski area. The track leads to the bottom of the 'Quad Chair'. Go past this chairlift and continue contouring WSW until overlooking the Allt Daim, the long glen separating Aonach Mòr and the peaks of Càrn Mòr Dearg. From the vicinity of a large cairn, descend into the glen, quickly veering left/S, down a natural but vague shelf line.

Three ridges drop down the otherwise barren slopes on the opposite side of the glen. The middle ridge has three large towers that form the mainstay of its crest. This is the east ridge of Càrn Dearg Meadhonach. Head up the floor of the glen until it seems appropriate to strike uphill towards the base of the ridge, the best line being down to the snow conditions on the day.

The bleak east flank of Càrn Mòr Dearg, with the east ridge of Càrn Dearg Meadhonach at its centre

Càrn Dearg Meadhonach East Ridge

The gondola uplift onto Aonach Mòr at the Nevis Range ski area

Reaching the top of the east ridge, with the large west face of Aonach Mòr behind - Steve Worth

Càrn Dearg Meadhonach East Ridge

At first the ridge is broad and ill defined. The lower slopes gradually merge to a fine arête, whose crest is a jumble of large, angular granite blocks. Enjoyable scrambling along the crest leads easily over the first tower to a short dip. The ridge is now exposed on both sides, considerably so to the north.

The second and main tower is also climbed direct, in an exposed and dramatic situation. From the top of the tower, descend slightly to the left/S side and then continue across a long, sweeping saddle to the third and smallest tower; the summit mound of Càrn Dearg Meadhonach. The views across to the Ben ensure that no gobs remain un-smacked.

Return If it's looking tight for making it back to the ski area for the last gondola (the time of the day's last ride is displayed at the top station), a bailout option is to head NW down the broad summit ridge towards Càrn Beag Dearg (1010m); the lowest of the mountain's tops. Continue over Càrn Beag Dearg and descend N to a flattening at 730m. From here, drop E into the Allt Daim and pick up the shelf line on the opposite side of the glen that leads up to the ski area.

To continue as planned, head SW from the summit of Càrn Dearg Meadhonach for 200m, before veering to the SSE and ascending the striking but easy walking ridge that leads to the summit of Càrn Mòr Dearg. Now descend the mountain's cool east ridge, a beautiful snow arête that curves down to the bealach at the head of the Allt Daim. The arête is straightforward and never quite steep enough to make grade I terrain. From its base, head NW down the glen and retrace the approach route back to the ski area.

If you've blown it attempting to make it back in time for the last gondola, continue down the Allt Daim, following the stream as far as a dam (NN 167 757). From the dam, pick up a forestry track, which initially descends W before veering around to the NE and contouring through forestry plantation. The track turns sharply back on itself at a junction (NN 166 766), from where it does a couple of long zig-zags downhill. Taking the right-hand fork at any subsequent junctions leads back to the ski area car park.

Càrn Dearg Meadhonach East Ridge
Ben Nevis Càrn Mòr Dearg Arête

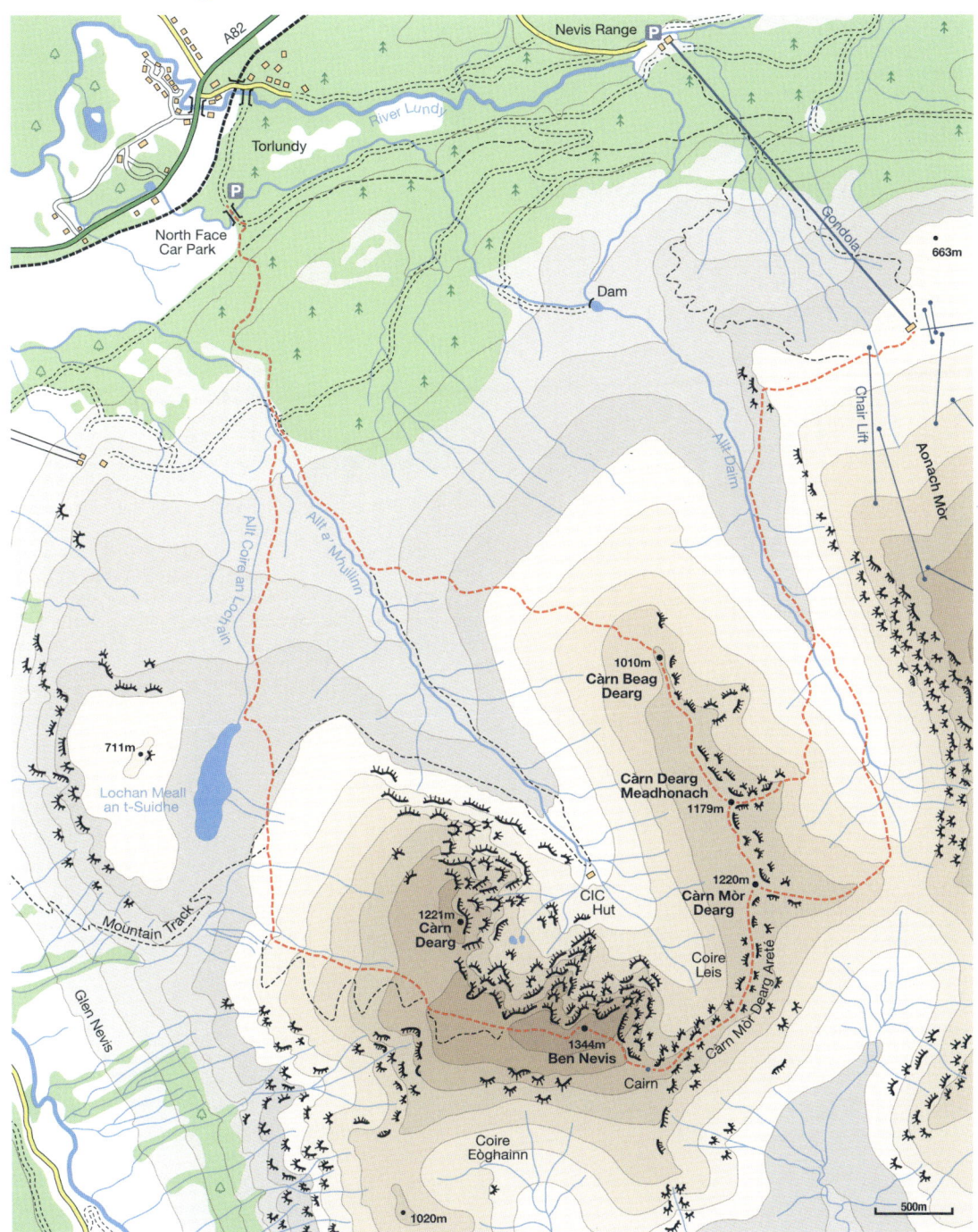

22 Ben Nevis Càrn Mòr Dearg Arête

A mid-January day on the Càrn Mòr Dearg Arête - Karen McIntyre

area
Fort William, West Highlands

start
NN 144 763

difficulty
Grade I

distance
15.4km

total ascent
1550m

maps
pages 111 & 124

A long and spectacular excursion This classic high-level journey takes in mountain scenery of an immense scale. Involving over 3km of exhilarating ridge walking and easy scrambling, it is an excellent way to reach the top of Ben Nevis. It is best reserved for when there's a chance of some clear weather.

Although not technically difficult, this is a big day and physically demanding. It can be attempted in any snow conditions, so long as there is no variation from the described descent route. Traversing the arête would be time consuming under deep powder or in a heavily iced condition. It is a complete no-goer if there is the potential for high winds.

Ben Nevis Càrn Mòr Dearg Arête

Background The long Allt a' Mhuilinn glen lies at the centre of a vast horseshoe formed by the joining of two very different mountains. The northeast side of the glen is enclosed by the streamlined bulk of Càrn Mòr Dearg (1220m). Rising steeply on the southwest side is the huge array of buttresses and ridges that form the north face of Ben Nevis (1344m). A narrow 1.4km-long ridge sweeps around the head of the glen connecting the two mountains; this is the Càrn Mòr Dearg Arête.

There are two good ways of getting to know Ben Nevis. The intimate way is by venturing into its north face, and climbing the mountain by one of its great ridges or easy gullies. The other option is by viewing Ben Nevis from the summit ridge of Càrn Mòr Dearg, high up on the opposite side of the Allt a' Mhuilinn. A walk along this ridge will reveal every nuance of the north face. And only by continuing across the Càrn Mòr Dearg Arête can the true nature and magnificence of the Ben's northeast buttress be properly appreciated.

The winter traverse of the Càrn Mòr Dearg Arête isn't difficult in terms of Scottish mountaineering. However, in poor snow conditions it can be a committing undertaking. Between the summit of Càrn Mòr Dearg and the top of the zig-zags on the Ben's Mountain Track (the path up from Glen Nevis), there may be only one opportunity to abandon the route with any degree of safety. And even that would be a very tricky exercise in poor visibility.

Description Start from the large North Face Car Park (NN 144 763) at Torlundy. The access road for the car park is located 4km northeast of Fort William on the A82, at a clearly sign-posted turn-off. From the turn-off, continue straight over a hump-backed bridge and then turn immediately right, again well sign-posted. Continue along a rough vehicle track for 800m to the car park.

From the southeast tip of the car park, go over a small bridge. Continue ahead for 100m, before taking a well-signed path on the right, which climbs steeply through the forestry. The path eventually joins a vehicle track that runs alongside the Allt a' Mhuilinn; the name of both the river and the long glen running beneath the north face of Ben Nevis. Head up the track to a small parking area and cross a large stile (NN 148 749). Now follow the well-made Allt a' Mhuilin path SE, towards the head of the glen.

From around 700m beyond the stile, break left/ESE from the path and start the long ascent towards Càrn Beag Dearg (1010m), the lowest and most northerly of Càrn Mòr Dearg's three tops. There is a vague trail somewhere, but it is easily obscured by snow and its usefulness in winter is debatable. The climb up the featureless hillside is hard going but invigorating and the small cairn at the centre of the summit mound is likely to be a welcome sight.

Crossing the summit ridge of Càrn Mòr Dearg with the northeast buttress of Ben Nevis as a backdrop - Karen McIntyre

Ben Nevis Càrn Mòr Dearg Arête

Strike SSE along the 2km-long high-level ridge that firstly stretches over Càrn Dearg Meadhonach (1179m) before gradually rising up to Càrn Mòr Dearg's highest top (1221m). From the mountain's triangular summit, head easily down the well-defined S spur. The spur soon narrows and its crest becomes littered with large, angular granite blocks; this is the beginning of the Càrn Mòr Dearg Arête. The arête is wonderfully airy with long sweeping slopes dropping on both sides. Only on a few short sections is it 'properly exposed'. Scrambling along its crest is straightforward, continuously flowing and in a magnificent situation.

At around 300m beyond the lowest point of the arête, at a flattening before the final climb towards Ben Nevis, a large cairn (NN 171 710) marks an old descent route into Coire Leis (on the right/north). The descent is sketchy in anything other than primo conditions (when the snow is both safe and easy to kick-in). It is a steep and frequently icy grade I slope, which only eases after dropping 150m.

It is also possible to descend left/south from the cairn, towards Glen Nevis. This has its own problems, especially in poor visibility. An initial grid bearing of 220 degrees will put you into the bowl of Coire Eòghainn but not into safety. From here, care is needed climbing down the steep ground on the true-left/east side of the burn (the Waterslide) that drops into Glen Nevis.

From the cairn, an ascent of 210m now follows, up a long, uniform snow slope leading onto the summit plateau. Dig deep. Be conscious that the edge to the right, overlooking Coire Leis, will invariably be corniced. The summit is located some 150m beyond the change in angle marking the edge of the plateau. In a harsh winter, the summit trig point can be completely buried by snow. However, the ruined observatory, located some 15m south of the summit, is an unmistakable feature. It is topped by a weather-tight shelter that can be used in emergencies.

Return In good visibility, the descent from the summit plateau is straightforward. A pleasant stroll in fact. It is easy to take a wide berth around the tops of the north face gullies and amble in a general WNW direction down the plateau's gentle slopes. A line of 2m-high cairns, spaced 50m apart, lead to the point where the Mountain Track meets the plateau. Continue in the same direction for a further 1km, down easy snow slopes, to around the 700m contour. From here, head N along the Mountain Track towards Lochan Meall an t-Suidhe.

More often than not, it is possible to take a short cut down the steep ground on the true-left bank of the Red Burn, situated just to the north of the Mountain Track zig-zags. In favourable snow conditions, these slopes provide a top class bum-slide. Be aware that the catchment area around the head of the burn is not immune from avalanche.

From a junction where the Mountain Track turns southwest towards Glen Nevis, follow a well-made path N to the northern end of Lochan Meall an t-Suidhe, also known as the Halfway Lochan. Keep to the true-right of the outflow and follow a vague track N across boggy ground. An old fence line is a useful navigation aid. Cross the Allt a' Mhuilinn at a weir (usually by clinging to the deer fencing), just below the small parking area. Retrace the approach route to the North Face Car Park.

Getting down from Ben Nevis in poor visibility has a reputation, and rightly so. In severe conditions it can be well gnarly finding the top of the Mountain Track, the one safe route off the plateau. It seems customary, and sensible, for guidebooks to supply precise navigational information for descending Ben Nevis. By doing this, it doesn't imply that getting off other big Scottish mountains in wild weather isn't also a serious proposition. So here goes…

From the summit trig point, follow a grid bearing of 230 degrees for 150m. This gets you clear of Gardyloo Gully, which bites into the plateau from the right/north. Then head downhill on a grid bearing of 280 degrees for over 800m, which will put you in the middle of the zig-zags at the top of the Mountain Track. Now continue downhill in the same direction on a noticeably steeper slope for a further 1km, to around the 700m contour. Then turn N and head towards the Halfway Lochan.

It is important to be spot on when following the line of these bearings, as a danger also comes from the steep crags around Five Finger Gully, which lies immediately south of the Mountain Track. If after pacing 800m on the second bearing you come to alarmingly steep ground, you have strayed too far to the left/south (a natural tendency in wanting to stay clear of the north face cliffs). If so, walk N uphill, until it is possible to continue safely on a 280 degrees bearing. A large-scale map of the plateau area showing the line of these bearings is on page 124.

Approaching the summit of Càrn Mòr Dearg on an eerie early February day - Dave Lees, Stevie Butterworth & Dom Fawcett

23 Ben Nevis Ledge Route

The exquisite final section of snow arête leading up to Càrn Dearg - Steve Worth

area
Fort William, West Highlands

start
NN 144 763

difficulty
Grade II

distance
12.7km

total ascent
1185m

maps
pages 124 & 111

An unlikely yet excellent mountaineering route A sneaky start leads onto a sequence of sloping ledges, which allow passage across the steep southeast flank of Càrn Dearg Buttress. Once the top of the buttress is gained, the nature of the route changes dramatically and a fine arête, in a spectacular situation, is followed up to the Ben's summit plateau.

An ascent of Ledge Route hinges upon there being stable snow conditions in Number 5 Gully, the lower section of which is unavoidable during the approach. The grade is a reflection of how serious the route can be rather than any technical difficulty. However, it still has its moments. It is a committing route, with no easy escape options beyond the second ledge.

Ben Nevis Ledge Route

Background There is often a misconception, or perhaps a snobby belief, that there are only four ridges on Ben Nevis that warrant 'classic' status; these being Tower Ridge, Castle Ridge and Observatory Ridge along with the crest of the Northeast Buttress. All of them, without question, are striking mountaineering lines. Perhaps because of its minimal difficulty and perhaps due to its non ridge-like name, Ledge Route somehow gets overlooked and is rarely included in the list. This is a surprise, because it is brilliant.

Ben Nevis has two main tops. The mountain's true summit (1344m) is at the eastern end of the plateau and is the site of the now ruined observatory. The second top, Càrn Dearg (1221m) is a 1.4km walk to the northwest, at the opposite end of the plateau, where it overlooks Fort William. It is from Carn Dearg that the fine arête of Ledge Route drops towards the Allt a' Mhuilinn glen. However, the arête doesn't drop the full extent of the north face; it stops abruptly, on the top of the huge and seemingly impregnable Càrn Dearg Buttress.

Reaching the base of the arête from the Allt a' Mhuilinn involves wandering across some improbable looking ground that should be far more difficult than it actually is. It is this unlikely line, and the way it meanders easily through magnificent and imposing terrain, which makes Ledge Route an absolute classic of a mountain journey.

Description Start from the North Face Car Park (NN 144 763) at Torlundy and follow the description of Route 22 (page 113), as far as the small parking area at the edge of the forestry (NN 148 749). From here, cross a large stile and follow the well-made Allt a' Mhuilinn path SE, towards the head of the glen. Approximately 3.5km along the path, at 680m, is an alpine-type mountain hut, the CIC Hut. The hut is privately owned and its facilities are not open to the public. On the whole, the occupants will be down to earth and have no proprietary views regarding Ben Nevis.

From about 150m before reaching the hut, at a point where the path is still level with the burn, cross over to the far/west bank. Head SW up an eroded track, towards the left-hand end of a rocky bluff, the Cascade Crags, which run rightwards up the hillside. Once around the toe of the bluff, veer W and head directly uphill over easy ground. Towering ahead is the unmistakable Carn Dearg Buttress, by far the largest and most prominent buttress in this area of the north face. To its left is the much smaller Moonlight Gully Buttress. Between them lies the entrance to Number 5 Gully. The layout is easily scoped from the vicinity of the hut.

In its upper part, Number 5 Gully opens out into a small bowl-shaped corrie that collects vast amounts of snow. The likely presence of old debris spread beneath the gully's base will give an indication of not only how often avalanches occur within Number 5 but also of their frightening size.

A team heading for the narrow entrance of Number 5 Gully, to the left of Càrn Dearg Buttress

Ben Nevis Ledge Route

The start of the snow arête, high above the Allt a' Mhuilinn on an alpine-like day in late March - Steve Worth

Descending towards the Red Burn in sublime conditions following an ascent of Ledge Route in early February - Gareth Jones and Nick Carver

Dropping into Number 4 Gully after an ascent of Ledge Route - Steve Worth

Continue to zig-zag uphill and enter Number 5 Gully (NN 162 721). About 50m beyond the initial narrowing, break out from the gully on the right, via a rightward-slanting ramp. The ramp leads to an almost horizontal ledge that sneaks right, across the southeast flank of Carn Dearg Buttress. Just before the ledge fades out, cut back left and ascend a leftward-leaning gully. This leads up to a second, slightly wider, snowy ledge.

Head right, along this second snowy ledge. At its far end, by a large, improbably balanced pinnacle, go round a corner to reach a sizeable platform nestled at the very top of Carn Dearg Buttress. This is a good place to pause for a while and comfortably take in the enormity of the surroundings.

Above the platform are the beginnings of a narrow, rocky ridge. There are no route finding issues from here on; simply follow the exposed crest with interest. The upper part of the ridge regularly forms into a long snowy arête, which snakes up to the northwest summit of Carn Dearg (1214m) and onto the summit plateau. Lovely.

The summit of Ben Nevis is now some 1.7km away at the eastern end of the plateau. Reaching it is an easy walk involving another 220m of ascent. On a clear day, simply follow the edge of the plateau around to the S, then E, giving a wide berth to the corniced edge. In poor visibility, don't wing it. Get your compass out and start pacing.

Return The most interesting way down from the plateau, which will complement the ascent, is via the extremely scenic Number 4 Gully. From Càrn Dearg's northwest summit (the top of Ledge Route), follow the edge of the plateau around to the S and cross over the gentle dome of Càrn Dearg's main summit (1221m). Just before the ground starts to rise again, a large gully cuts deeply into the plateau. This is Number 4. A well-constructed, 1.5m-high cairn will confirm where you are (NN 158 717).

Occasionally the extent of the cornice around the top of Number 4 can pose problems and an abseil may be the only way to safely gain the gully. With a 30m rope, a snow bollard will be the only anchor available. Sometimes, the cornice is so large that it is impassable. If a change of plan is required, heading 300m in a WSW direction places you at the top of the Red Burn catchment area. From here, the Mountain Track descent route can be followed back to the Allt a' Mhuilinn, as described on page 114.

Having negotiated any cornice, the descent of Number 4 Gully is straightforward. The enclosed gully soon opens out to broad uniform slopes, which at their greatest extent stretch for over 250m around the head of Coire na Ciste. Keep to the true-left on these slopes while descending, aiming for the left/west side of the lochan. Beyond the lochan, stay on the left/west side of the burn and follow this down to the CIC Hut, from where the Allt a' Mhuilinn path is gained. Or, from approximately 250m before reaching the hut, where the ground dictates, take a more direct line and head NW to pick up the path further down the glen.

24 Ben Nevis South Castle Gully

The steep exit slopes to South Castle Gully - Dave McGimpsey

area
Fort William, West Highlands

start
NN 144 763

difficulty
Grade I/II

distance
12.4km

total ascent
1185m

maps
pages 124 & 111

A remarkable gully in a quiet corner of Ben Nevis This exceptional outing climbs out of the Castle Coire bowl onto the mountain's northwest shoulder and is steeped in atmosphere; impressive rock architecture surrounds the entire ascent. It is a relatively short excursion in terms of mountaineering on the Ben.

A huge chockstone at the gully's entrance can prove to be an impassable crux. An ascent in the latter part of the season is often better, when the gully is more likely to be filled-in and the chockstone buried. Otherwise, the neighbouring North Castle Gully can save the day. The entire Castle Coire area is highly prone to avalanche, so being certain of stable snow conditions is an absolute must.

Ben Nevis South Castle Gully

Background When heading up the Allt a' Mhuilinn glen, the first main feature of the north face, seen up on the right, is the steep line of Castle Ridge and its extensive north flanking wall. Beyond, further to the left, is the huge Carn Dearg Buttress; an unmistakable, 300m-high prow of compact rock, from whose top the fine arête of Ledge Route can be seen curving up to the summit plateau. The large recessed area nestled between these two notable features is known as Castle Coire.

It is not until much further up the glen, approximately 500m before reaching the CIC Hut, that the layout of Castle Coire can be seen in its entirety. The corrie gets its name from the isolated, wedge-shaped buttress that stands proudly at its head. The buttress is flanked by two deep and narrow gullies, South Castle Gully on the left and North Castle Gully on the right. Despite being the first corrie encountered along the Allt a' Mhuilinn, and being relatively straightforward to reach, it is strangely one of the least visited on Ben Nevis.

It is important to be sure of a minimal avalanche risk before heading into the Castle Coire area. Huge avalanches regularly sweep the corrie and its approach routes; this is a given following heavy snowfall. A 'go and have a look' tactic won't cut it here as there is nowhere within the corrie that is safe. Bide your time, and enjoy South Castle Gully when you're certain it will contain firm, stress-free snow. After all, it is the best easy gully on the Ben.

Description Start from the North Face Car Park (NN 144 763) at Torlundy and follow the description of Route 22 (page 113), as far as the small parking area at the edge of the forestry (NN 148 749). From here, cross a large stile and follow the well-made Allt a' Mhuilinn path SE, towards the head of the glen. After around 3km (roughly 500m before reaching the CIC Hut), once Castle Coire has come into view, cross to the southwest bank of the Allt a' Mhuilinn stream. If the stream is high, crossing nearer to the hut will be easier, above two significant tributaries.

On the southwest side of the stream, go up the easy apron slopes then ascend a rightward-leaning snow ramp that cuts through the band of bluffs guarding the base of Castle Coire. If approaching from near the hut, it is more practical to head W uphill, to where a traverse NW can be made along the wide sloping terrace that runs beneath Càrn Dearg Buttress. Both approaches place you in the snow bowl at the centre of Castle Coire. Now zig-zag up the steep snow slopes towards the rear of the corrie, to reach the narrow entrance to South Castle Gully.

Heading for the Red Burn across the west flank of Càrn Dearg - Dave McGimpsey

A team approaching the access ramp leading into Castle Coire with South Castle Gully starting from the centre of the snowfield

Ben Nevis South Castle Gully

South Castle Gully is long (220m), enclosed and extremely atmospheric. With a decent build-up of snow it will be a straightforward snow climb, on the cusp between grade I and II. However, if the infamous chockstone is visible, spanning the mouth of the gully (it is the size of a van), there is a strong likelihood it will be impassable. Only if there is a strip of helpful snow on the narrow ramp running up the chockstone's left-hand side, are you still in with a fighting chance. Otherwise, skulk off to the right, beneath the Castle, and head up North Castle Gully instead.

North Castle Gully is also a fantastic climb, just a little less atmospheric than its neighbour. That said if it were on any other west coast mountain, it would be the first choice route. It is marginally steeper but still climbable in lean conditions (the gully has two chockstones of its own that create awkward but not insurmountable steps). It would be rare for either gully to have a large cornice, or at least one that couldn't be out-flanked.

Return From the promontory at the top of South Castle Gully (a short distance above the exit of North Castle Gully), head SE up easy ground towards the summit of Càrn Dearg (1221m). From the summit, or earlier, veer SW towards the catchment area of the Red Burn, from where the Mountain Track descent route can be followed back to the Allt a' Mhuilinn, as described on page 114.

When there is continuous and stable snow cover down to Lochan Meall an t-Suidhe, an easy descent can be made directly down the north side of Carn Dearg. From the top of South Gully, head W for 300m, to avoid the north flank of Castle Ridge, then bail straight down the slope to the lochan. Without decent snow cover, descending this boulder-covered slope is a nightmare and is not recommended.

Ben Nevis Ledge Route
Ben Nevis South Castle Gully

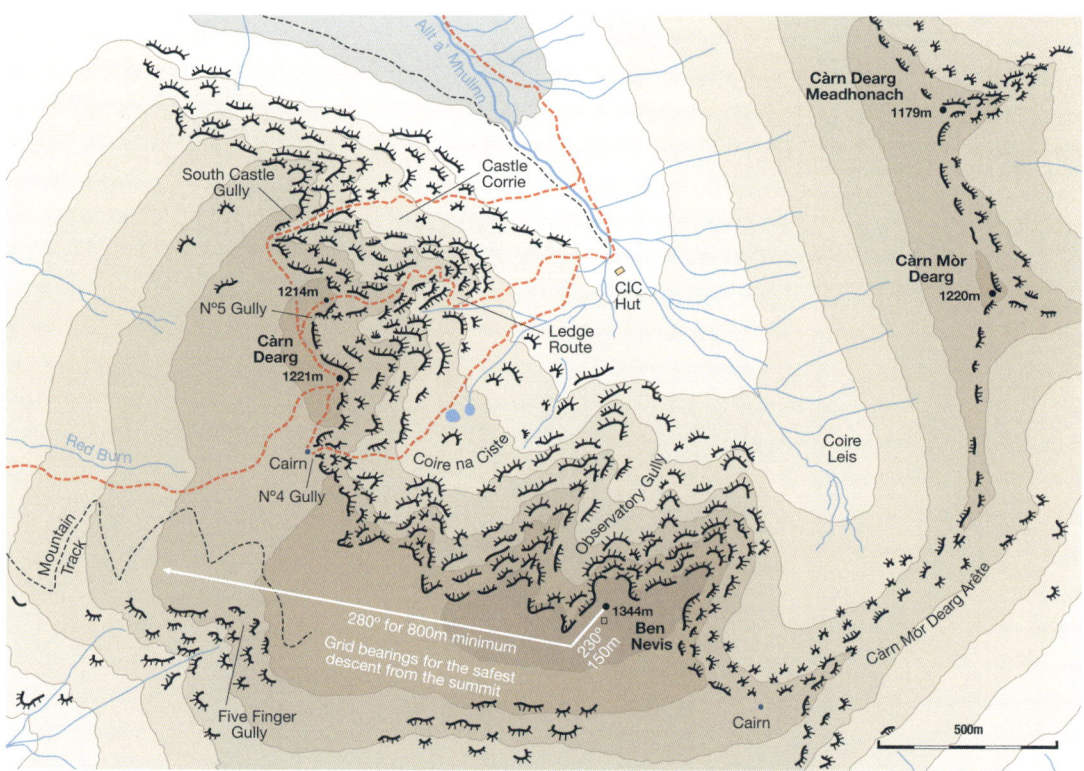

25 Stob Bàn South Gully

South Gully on a cold mid-February morning - Ian Hey

area
Fort William,
West Highlands

start
NN 145 683

difficulty
Grade I

distance
8.8km

total ascent
1075m

map
page 128

A quality route up the Mamores' most attractive peak Everything about this reads like a wish list for an easy mountaineering day; a pleasant approach on a lovely path, an incredibly scenic snow gully, a sharp summit with tremendous views and an airy ridge for the descent. And all the time remaining well within the threshold of grade I.

South Gully faces northeast and holds snow reasonably well. In suspect snow conditions, ascending Stob Bàn by its east ridge would still make for a rewarding traverse; full of mountaineering flavour and again staying within grade I. A longer, alternative return route is also possible, taking in the nearby 'Devil's Ridge'.

Stob Bàn South Gully

Background Stob Bàn (999m) is situated 9km southeast of Fort William at the western end of the Mamores, the long chain of sharp peaks that lie between Glen Nevis and Loch Leven. It is a striking mountain, particularly when seen from lower Glen Nevis, the starting point for this journey. There are four main ridges, three of which drop directly from Stob Bàn's pointed summit, giving the mountain its classic pyramid shape. Its north ridge descends towards Glen Nevis, splitting as it does so, to form the mountain's fourth ridge, which extends east to connect with the nearby Mullach nan Coirean (939m).

The Mamores are perhaps best known for their narrow interconnecting ridges, which allow high-level walking circuits that can take in a number of the range's peaks in a single outing. In winter, these shapely peaks become top-end winter hillwalking terrain; their ridges being dramatic and airy but not quite crossing the threshold to warrant a technical classification… though what's in a label! There are of course exceptions, and one of these is Stob Bàn's north ridge.

Stob Bàn stands out within the Mamores, not just because of its distinctive summit cone but also for its impressive northeast cliffs, whose laid-back buttresses and gullies contain an attractive selection of mountaineering lines. The easiest of these lines, and leading directly to the summit, is South Gully. Its ascent, when combined with a descent of the mountain's north ridge, gives a contrasting twist to a traverse of this classic Mamores peak.

Description Start at the Lower Falls Car Park next to where the Glen Nevis road crosses the River Nevis (NN 145 683), 300m east of Achriabhach. Follow a good path SE towards Coire a' Mhusgain. For just under 2.5km the path stays a short distance above the east bank of the river, the Allt Coire a' Mhusgain, before zig-zagging steeply up the hillside on the left/NE. It then traverses SE across the open hillside, towards the head of the glen. The traverse is directly opposite Stob Ban's northeast cliffs and is a good place to stop for an un-obscured scope of their layout.

Looking across the glen, the lowest buttress, on the right, is North Buttress. The impressive triangular-shaped crag, set forward in the centre of the cliffs, is Central Buttress. The long buttress on the left of the cliffs, South Buttress, is split by two prominent snow gullies. The straight right-hand gully is North Gully, The curving left-hand gully is South Gully.

In favourable snow conditions, when walking off the path is easy going, a direct approach to the base of South Gully is an aesthetic if energetic option. Leave the path (NN 155 660 is probably the best point) and descend to the burn. Cross over and then pick a way W up to a flattening, before ascending SW up steep slopes to the gully's entrance (NN 148 655).

The northeast cliffs of Stob Bàn with South Gully curving left from the centre of the snowfield

Stob Bàn South Gully

Alternatively, continue SE up the path, into a wide bowl at the head of the glen. Climb SW out of the bowl, then head NE and climb onto the lower shoulder of Stob Bàn's east ridge. At a point where the ridge meets with the left/east edge of South Buttress, descend steeply NW, then traverse W, beneath the cliffs of South Buttress, to reach the entrance of South Gully. Head up the gully without any difficulty. At its top, scamper up to the nearby summit (999m).

Return Head down the narrow N ridge, usually a snow arête in its upper part. After 200m the ridge veers to the NW, dropping to a minor top (912m) and the junction with the east ridge. From this small top, head NNE across a snowy saddle, to a second and more pronounced minor top. From here, descend NW, scrambling down much steeper ground than has been descended so far. This eventually leads onto a large flat area.

Head NNW across the flat area and then continue easily down the now broad N ridge for a further 1km, to where it noticeably steepens. To avoid some steep bluffs, descend NW via a short and very easy scramble of no more than 50m. A faint zig-zag path then leads down into an area of woodland regeneration. Follow the path N to the Glen Nevis road, arriving a short distance west of the start point.

An early morning approach up Coire a' Mhusgain and first light on Stob Bàn's northeast cliffs - Ian Hey

Stob Bàn South Gully

An alternative return route, more like an extension, is to traverse the peaks on the west side of Coire a' Mhusgain and therefore cross the ominously named Devil's Ridge. This is a beautifully chiselled and wonderfully airy stretch of ridge running over the spine of Stob a' Choire Mhail and connecting with Sgùrr a' Mhàim. Its name perhaps exaggerates its difficulty.

From the summit of Stob Bàn, drop steeply S for 20m then descend the well-defined E ridge to a shoulder at 805m. From here, drop SE down a short flanking slope, then head E to the lochan nestled in the small bowl of Coire nam Miseach. In poor visibility this is confusing terrain, with harmless snow banks contriving to mimic edges. From the lochan, zig-zag up to the wide col beneath the south ridge of Stob a' Choire Mhail and the start of the Devil's Ridge.

Head N up the attractively narrow ridge, which is straightforward and without exposure. From the sharp summit (990m) continue N, down the crest of a fine arête. A very short section of easy scrambling bypasses a leaning pinnacle on the left/W. Beyond a small notch, easy slopes lead NE up to a small shoulder on Sgùrr a' Mhàim. A short, blunt ridge then leads easily up to the summit cairn (1099m).

From the summit, descend NNW, down a well-defined ridge that quickly veers to the N. At 1000m, break off to the left/NW, down straightforward, gentle slopes. Continue descending in this direction to where the ground merges into a broad spur, with bluffs on the right/northeast. A vague path now zig-zags down open ground to meet with the Coire a' Mhusgain path used on the approach… and so to Glen Nevis.

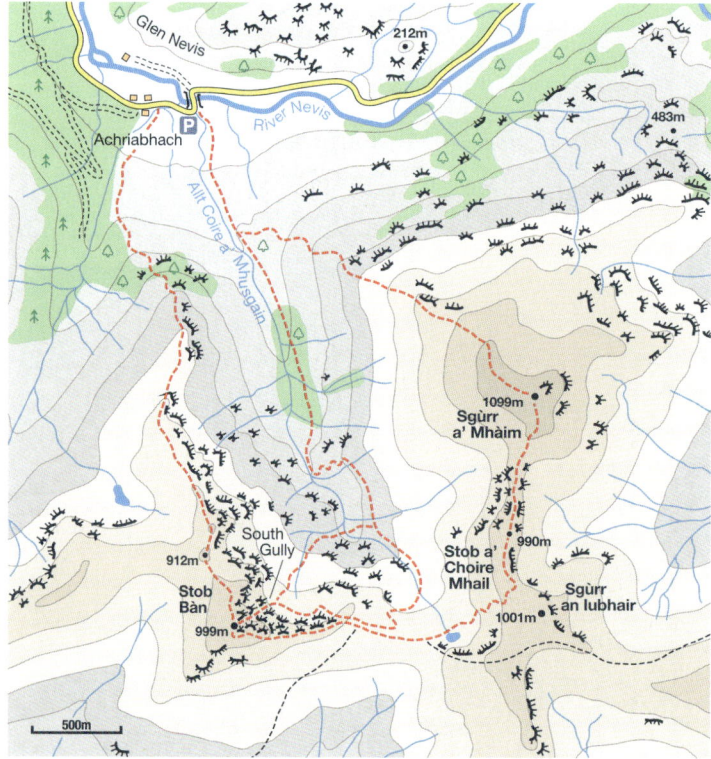

26 Beinn a' Bheithir The Two Ridges

The final exposed rock step on Schoolhouse Ridge - Paul James

area
Balachulish, West Highlands

start
NN 084 585

difficulty
Grade I

distance
9.4km

total ascent
995m

map
page 133

Two striking ridges on a big west coast hill This natural link-up gives a very good and relatively straightforward mountaineering day. Schoolhouse Ridge, the lower ridge, requires a bit of oomph to get over a couple of exposed rocky steps, otherwise it is an easy winter scramble. There are no difficulties on the second ridge; it is simply a leisurely tootle up a spectacular snowy arête.

Despite Beinn a' Bheithir's size this is not a big outing, mainly due to the quick approach from Ballachulish. Both ridges are a safe option in all snow conditions, as is the descent with a slight detour. The expansive summit views are hard to match hereabouts.

Beinn a' Bheithir The Two Ridges

Background Beinn a' Bheithir (1024m) is a grand mountain that stands on its own, overlooking the narrows at the seaward end of Loch Leven. Its eye-catching ridges emanate from three prominent summits creating a double horseshoe-shaped range. Viewed from the north or the east, two of these ridges are especially attractive. They are both pure, unbroken lines and cry out to be climbed as soon as they are seen.

The lower of these ridges is the east-northeast spur of Beinn a' Bheithir's eastern most top, Sgorr Bhan. Owing to its position directly behind Ballachulish Primary School, it is known simply as Schoolhouse Ridge. Its well-defined crest maintains a fairly uniform angle as it soars up from Gleann an Fhiodh to the shoulder of Sgorr Bhan. It provides a dramatic and airy route onto the main horseshoe.

The natural continuation from Schoolhouse Ridge is the west ridge of Sgorr Dhearg, the higher of Beinn a' Bheithir's two Munros. Aesthetically this is one of Scotland's finest snowy ridges; sweeping, elegant and usually snow-covered throughout most of the season. The ridge has no exposure and is never quite steep enough to cause concerns about snow stability. In addition, cornices only ever form on its northern side and can easily be avoided. This is a snowy ridge for all the people.

Description Start in Ballachulish just off the A82 (NN 084 585), 2km west of Glencoe village. There is a car park adjacent to the tourist information centre. Walk S through the village and follow the lane on the west side of the River Laroch to the end of the tarmac road, 150m beyond the primary school. Continue S along the track (way-marked for Glen Creran) to reach a gate after 900m. The slender crest of Schoolhouse Ridge dominates the view to the right.

From the gate, follow a faint track SW across open ground. The path takes a more-or-less direct line to the broad base of the ridge, before zig-zagging up the left/south flank onto the first semblance of a crest. Head up the ridge, picking a way over small outcrops without any difficulty. On the final narrow section of the ridge there are two steep and exposed steps. In most snow conditions it is best to climb these direct. Probing and clearing will reveal helpful quartzite ledges. The top of the second step pops out onto the broad northeast spur of Sgorr Bhan, giving a sudden finish to the ridge.

From the top of Schoolhouse Ridge, walk SW, up to Sgorr Bhan's rocky summit (947m) and the first unobscured view of Sgorr Dhearg's exquisite snow arête. A short descent SW over blocky ground leads onto a long, flat col. Now stroll up one of the best snowy ridges in Scotland to reach the summit trig point and 360 degree views.

The superb snow arête on Sgorr Dhearg's west ridge - Paul James

On the lower shoulder of Schoolhouse Ridge - Paul James

Return The natural continuation would be to descend the long and gently angled north ridge, towards Loch Leven. However, the final 250m of height loss is through unbelievably crappy forestry plantation. Not something to look forward to at the end of a good day. Instead, head back down Sgorr Dhearg's snow arête (just as good in reverse) and re-trace the approach route over Sgorr Bhan. When nearing the top of Schoolhouse Ridge, bear NNW before turning NNE to descend towards Beinn Bhàn. In poor visibility a large wind scoop (nearly always present) can cause confusion at this intersection, as it can easily be mistaken for a cornice.

At the first significant flattening on the NE ridge, at 580m, break right and drop steeply into Coire Riabhach. Continue down either bank of the Allt á Choire Riabhaich to reconnect with the track leading to the Primary School. A less steep descent continues down the NE ridge to 390m, before cutting back in a SSE direction into Coire Riabhach. This would be a preferable route in heavy snow conditions.

A good, energetic extension to this journey is to take in the summit of Sgorr Dhonuill (1001m), the second Munro in the range. From the summit of Sgorr Dhearg, head down the well-defined and easy SW ridge, to reach the broad bealach between the two peaks. Now head W, again on an easy ridge, up to a level section (930m). Straightforward scrambling then leads to the small summit plateau. To return to Ballachulish, it is logistically more sensible and aesthetically better to retrace the route over Sgorr Dhearg, long as this may seem.

Cruisey winter scrambling on the upper crest of Schoolhouse Ridge - Paul James

Alternatively, return to the broad bealach and drop N, down easy slopes towards the forestry plantation. From the highest stand of trees, head NNE, along a rough path that stays a short distance above the edge of the forestry. After approximately 500m, just beyond a gate, the path leads into the trees (NN 051 567). From now on, the path is well made and easy going. It descends NNW, then briefly SW, to eventually reach a forestry track. Cross the track and continue descending on the path, first SW, then NNW (only the upper section of the path is marked on the Harvey's Glencoe map and it is completely omitted on the current OS map).

At the next junction, leave the path and turn right/NE onto a wide forestry track. Follow the track for just under 3.5km, ignoring any branch roads, as it contours around the north spur of Sgorr Dhearg. At the far side of the spur, where the track cuts sharply back to the left (NN 065 584), continue straight ahead on a footpath. The path skirts the boundary of a church ground before popping out on the A82, 1.5km west of the start point.

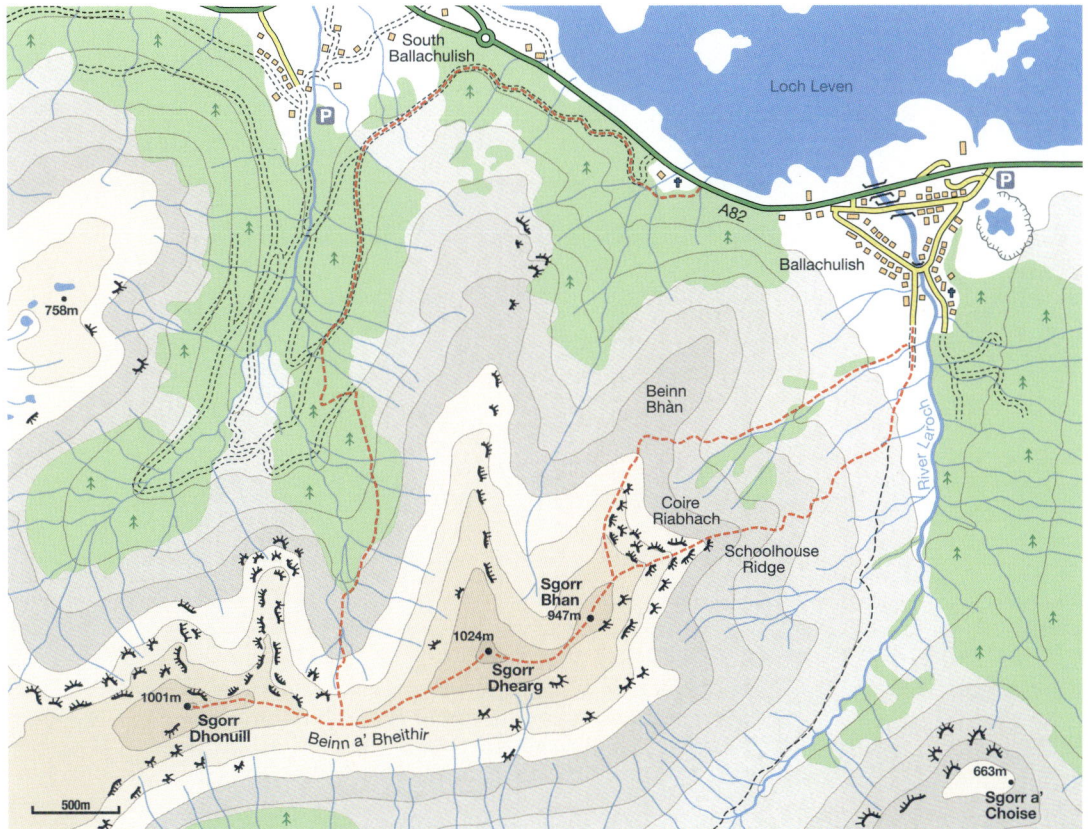

27 Aonach Eagach The Traverse

Crossing Meal Dearg on the Aonach Eagach traverse in early January - Steve Worth

area
Glencoe,
West Highlands

start
NN 173 567

difficulty
Grade II

distance
8.7km

total ascent
1240m

map
page 138

A life affirming expedition The winter traverse of this famous Glencoe ridge is a delight. It involves sustained and exposed scrambling over and around towers and pinnacles, narrow ledge shuffles, knife-edge gaps, tricky down-climbs and no shortage of snowy arêtes… all in the most magnificent surroundings. Most teams should expect to rope-up for some, if not all, of the difficulties.

This is a committing undertaking and moving quickly is a priority, especially at the beginning of the season with fewer daylight hours. Start early and don't underestimate the time it can take. The traverse is arguably best after heavy snowfall; the going may be trickier but the ridge will be at its most beautiful. There is little avalanche threat on the crest.

Aonach Eagach The Traverse

Background The Aonach Eagach, *Notched Ridge*, is the central part of the single ridgeline that stretches along the entire north side of Glencoe. Specifically, the name only applies to the highest and narrowest section of the ridgeline, which contains the peaks Am Bodach (943m), Meall Dearg (953m), Stob Coire Lèith (940m) and Sgòrr nam Fiannaidh (967m). Seen from the glen floor it is an impressive sight, but its true nature can only be appreciated from up high.

The Glencoe side of the Aonach Eagach has no corries, or rather none big enough to give it any kind of shape. It is effectively a great wall. Its near featureless lower slopes rise from the glen floor, in ever-increasing steepness, to support an array of rippled buttresses; themselves scored by numerous deep gullies. It is the sharp tops of the highest of these buttresses that form the serrated crest of the ridge. There is no safe descent on this side of the Aonach Eagach.

The north side of the Aonach Eagach is also a bugger to get off. Although more featured - there are two spurs projecting north - the terrain is equally intimidating and there are no safe ways down. There is an opportunity to descend near the western end of the ridge but it is not without difficulty and would be a desperate measure. If you run out of daylight on a traverse, it is better to persevere or reverse your steps over known terrain. This is one of the great winter mountaineering routes of Scotland, and not without reason. Treat it with respect regardless of your ability.

Description The traverse is described in the conventional east to west direction. Start at a small layby on the north side of the A82 in Glencoe (NN 173 567), 300m west of the bridge and white cottage at Allt-na-reigh. Follow the small signposted path that climbs steeply NE from the layby and weaves its way onto the broad southeast spur of Am Bodach. Head NW up the spur, which is steep with the occasional rocky outcrop. Higher up, beyond 800m, the spur loses definition and the angle eases. Straightforward slopes then lead directly to the summit of Am Bodach (943m), the easternmost peak of the Aonach Eagach.

Finding the way down from Am Bodach involves some sniffing around. When under powder, or when icy, it can feel decidedly sketchy. From the summit head WNW along the narrowing crest of the ridge, to where the ground suddenly drops off ahead. Scramble down an exposed sloping ledge on the right/N. At the end of the ledge, veer back left/S and down-climb a short, tricky corner/chimney, which leads back onto the crest. Continue along the now easy ridge to a minor un-named top (924m).

From the small cairn on the minor top, descend on the right/N and drop obliquely leftwards/NW, to reach a snowy col at the head of a deep gully. Now head NW up easy slopes, onto the broad summit dome of Meall Dearg (953m), the first of the Aonach Eagach's two Munros.

Following on from Am Bodach at the eastern end of the ridge - Steve Worth

Aonach Eagach The Traverse

From the summit of Meall Dearg, the view of the ridge ahead is superb; the crest sports an array of pointed buttresses, pinnacles and notches, whilst both flanks drop with intimidating steepness all the way to the glens below. From now on there are no route finding problems; simply follow your nose along the ridge. The crest is very exposed but the going is always steady. One awkward slabby descent may require an abseil. It is best to climb over 'The Pinnacles', two large rock spikes often considered the crux, rather than attempt to shuffle around them.

A distinctive col signals the end of the difficulties. From here a narrow and much easier ridge leads up to Stob Coire Lèith (940m). Leaving the small summit dome, a long and fairly level saddle connects to Sgorr nam Fiannaidh (967m), the Aonach Eagach's second Munro. Stroll across this lovely section of ridge for a fine end to the traverse and the widest views of the day from the summit wind-break.

Return By far the safest and least taxing way to descend is to head down the defined W ridge of Sgorr nam Fiannaidh. After 700m, veer NNW down Cnap Glas; the broad and uncomplicated shoulder that extends towards the Pap of Glencoe. From midway down the shoulder (after roughly 500m), bail WNW down a distinctive trough (NN 131 583). Otherwise, if snow conditions are poor, continue NNW into the deep col that separates Cnap Glas from the Pap. Either way, the descent is continued down a path on the true-left/south side of the Allt a' Mhuilinn, arriving at the road by the edge of the Invercoe forestry plantation (NN 110 585).

The Aonach Eagach traverse is undeniably easier to arrange if there are two vehicles involved. One of which can be left at the end of the ridge for a shuttle. There is a handy car park in the forestry plantation 500m SE of the Bridge of Glencoe (NN 107 587), only 400m from the described finish point.

Climbing up from Glencoe in early morning light, with the Bidean nam Bian massif behind - Steve Worth

Aonach Eagach The Traverse

The tricky and exposed descent of Am Bodach and the start of the difficulties - Steve Worth

Crossing the first of 'The Pinnacles' and nearing the end of the difficulties on the ridge - Steve Worth

Aonach Eagach The Traverse

Without the luxury of a second vehicle it is now some 7km back to the start point. This is firstly 2.5km SE along the single-track road to the Clachaig Inn (and the possibility of scoring a lift), then onwards for a further 1km to the A82. Although traffic is sparse in the winter, hitching is reasonably reliable as most drivers seem willing to stop. If it's late, consider walking 1.5km NW through Glencoe Village to the junction with the A82, where there will be a much better chance of a pick-up.

In safe snow conditions, an alternative descent, and posing less of a logistical problem, is through the shallow corrie directly south of Sgorr nam Fiannaidh. From a short distance W of the summit cairn, choose the best line and bail S down steep slopes. Stay a good distance from the true-left/east bank of the Allt an t-Sidhein, avoiding craggy ground where the stream converges with a tributary. This is not a pleasant way down.

To reiterate, there are no safe descent routes on the north side of the ridge. That's not to say descents aren't possible, they are just fraught with difficulty, especially in poor visibility. If needs must, the earliest sensible opportunity is from the col (815m, NN 151 583) at the base of the ridge leading up to Stob Coire Lèith. From here, drop N, trending initially right/NE, before skirting beneath the crags at the headwall of Coire Cam. Then descend directly down easier slopes into the corrie. Follow the true-right/east side of the Allt Gleann a' Chaolais to meet with a quad track lower down the glen (NN 154 599).

No matter how strong the pull of the Clachaig Inn, the old summer route on the west side of the Clachaig Gully/Gorge isn't recommended as a way down. It is a serious and dangerous descent in winter.

Aonach Eagach The Traverse

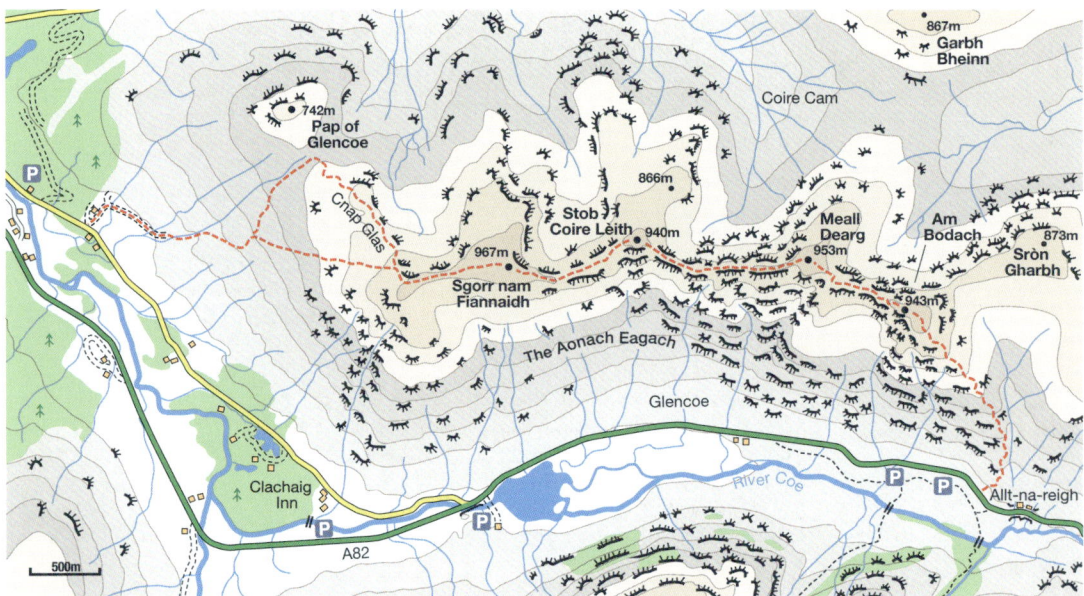

28 Stob Coire nam Beith Summit Gully

Descending the northeast shoulder of Bidean nam Bian, with Stob Coire nam Beith to the left - Steve Worth

area
Glencoe,
West Highlands

start
NN 138 566

difficulty
Grade I/II

distance
7.6km

total ascent
1300m

map
page 142

Proper Scottish winter mountaineering This long and sinuous gully finishes bang on the summit of a very attractive peak. It is a wonderful excursion in its own right but if combined with a crossing of Bidean nam Bian and Stob Coire nan Lochan, it makes for an exceptional journey through this intricate and compact massif.

The gully faces north and accumulates a lot of snow; it has large, enclosed catchment areas at its start, finish and central sections. Discretion is needed even when the same aspect is super stable elsewhere. It is an awkward gully to grade. When icy, one or two steep steps can feel at the upper end of grade II. In most snowy conditions the gully is likely to be a steep grade I. Or think of it this way, you wouldn't choose to descend it.

Stob Coire nam Beith Summit Gully

Background Bidean nam Bian is the complex massif that bounds the south side of Glencoe. Its name is more commonly used to identify its highest point but actually applies to the mountain as a whole, which includes a number of other significant peaks. The main ridge of the mountain forms a long north-facing arc, with the pronounced rocky summit of Bidean nam Bian (1150m) sitting at its centre. From here, a subsidiary Y-shaped ridge projects northwards, which itself supports a prominent peak at its centre; the shapely Stob Coire nan Lochan (1115m).

The ridges of Bidean nam Bian enclose three long corries that open towards Glencoe; Coire Gabhail, Coire nan Lochan and Coire nam Beitheach. They are equally impressive yet starkly different, each having an elaborate upper layout containing inner basins that are concealed from the glen. Any one of the corries makes an interesting approach into the massif. A through journey combining any two is highly recommended.

Stob Coire nam Beith (1107m) is the most westerly of Bidean's peaks and towers above the head of Coire nam Beitheach. Its 350m-high north face dominates the view from Glencoe over Loch Achtriochtan, presenting a dream mountaineering objective. The triangular face is riven with buttresses and crossed by a network of interconnecting gullies. The easiest and most obvious of these gullies runs the entire length of the face and leads directly to the summit. This is Summit Gully, by far the most scenic 'one axe' route onto Bidean's tops.

Description Start at a small car park on the south side of the A82 in Glencoe (NN 138 566), immediately east of the bridge over the River Coe and opposite the junction with the single-track road leading to the Clachaig Inn. Walk across the bridge and go through a gate at the end of the steel road barrier. Follow a good path S, which gradually steepens as the prominent waterfalls are approached. The path climbs over a short rock step (surprisingly tricky if icy!) before zig-zagging its way up the right/west side of the falls.

At the head of the zig-zags the path levels out into a short gorge at the entrance to Coire nam Beitheach. It then continues into the corrie, staying a short distance above the right/west bank of the gorge. If the path is iced, or obscured by snow, it may be easier to proceed at stream level. Where a huge boulder spans the gorge, cross to the left/east bank of the stream and continue up to a stream junction with three branches.

The stream junction is as good a spot as any to survey the corrie and is also a good reference spot from which to find Summit Gully in poor visibility. The gully runs up beneath the right-hand skyline of Stob Coire nam Beith and its wide entrance is the most significant gap in the base of the cliffs. If it can't be seen, head up the left/east bank of the vague central stream branch, which meanders up to the entrance of the gully (NN 138 550). In good visibility, just take the easiest line.

The north face of Stob Coire nam Beith, with the wide depression of Summit Gully on the right

In the easy lower reaches of Summit Gully - Ian Hey

Stob Coire nam Beith Summit Gully

The initial part of the gully is straightforward and incredibly scenic. At the first fork, beneath a pyramid-shaped tower, stick with the main easier-angled gully and ignore the steeper and narrower branch that climbs to the left of the tower. Various options now exist, the best being to head right at the next feasible opportunity, over a steep snowy step into an enclosed subsidiary branch. At the top of this hemmed-in branch, climb out to the left, onto a promontory that sits in the centre of the main gully. This dog-leg avoids an impassable cave pitch when there is insufficient build-up of snow.

From now on follow the line of least resistance, or better, the one that looks most attractive. The final slopes lead into a small bowl, where any cornice can be easily out-flanked. In firm conditions, the mixed ground either side of the upper gully can provide good variations, giving an uncharted and exploratory feel to the finish of the climb. All options arrive within a few metres of the summit cairn (1107m). Well cool.

Return The quickest and easiest descent is via the Bealach An t-Sròn. This is the col between Stob Coire nam Beith and An t-Sròn, the north-northwest spur of the mountain. From the summit cairn head W, skirting around the head of Summit Gully before descending the broad W ridge. The ridge soon becomes well-defined and begins to level-off as it curves to the N. Continue without difficulty down to the Bealach An t-Sròn (885m, NN 134 547), where a small hump separates the two lowest points.

From the bealach, bail E down straightforward snow slopes (steep at first) into upper Coire nam Beitheach. Continue N into the main corrie, being conscious in poor visibility of small outcrops in the middle of the slope. Lower down, staying well to the true-right/east side of the main stream avoids small bluffs around a deep gorge. Rejoin the approach path at the stream junction… and so to Glencoe.

Stob Coire nam Beith Summit Gully
Stob Coire Sgreamhach Sròn na Làirig

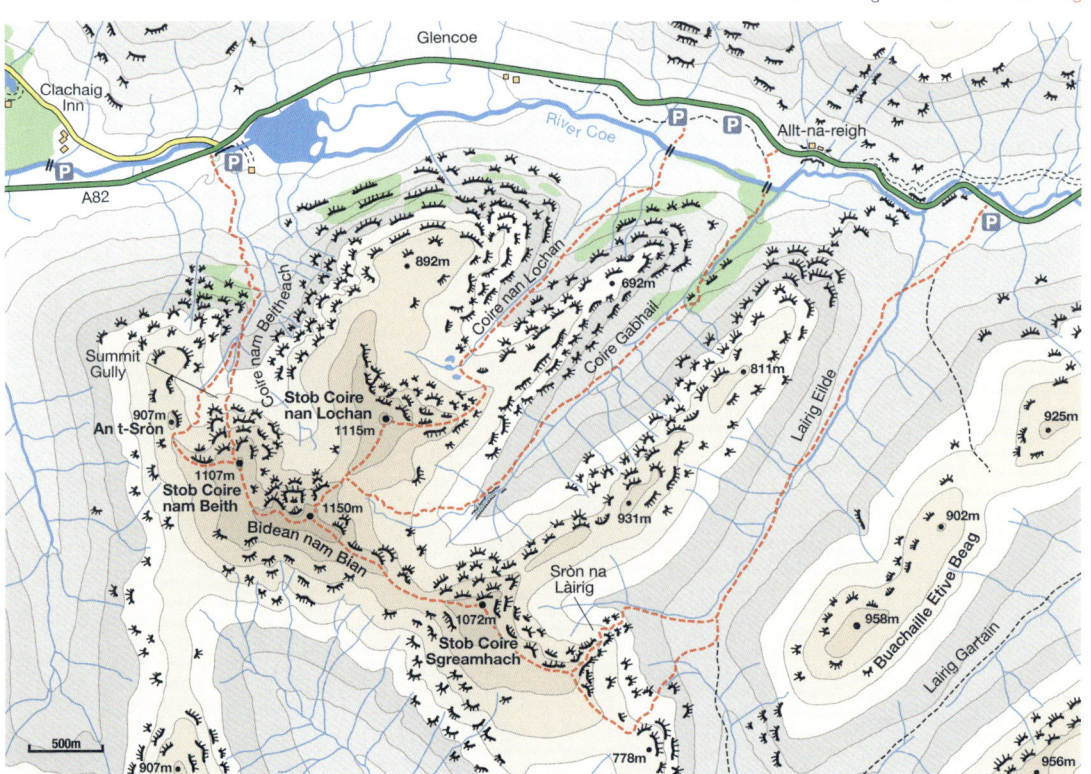

Stob Coire nam Beith Summit Gully

To continue on a journey through the massif, head SSE from the summit of Stob Coire nam Beith, down a well-defined ridge that leads onto a long saddle. The narrow crest of the saddle often forms a snow arête and curves up to the E to meet with the broad west top of Bidean nam Bian (1141m). A further short saddle stretches E to connect with the more pronounced main summit (1150m).

From Bidean nam Bian's main summit, head NE, down steep broken ground, to gain the top of a well-defined and level shoulder. Continuing north along the shoulder would culminate in a steep buttress, Diamond Buttress; so, from 50m before its end, drop easily right/NE onto a defined ridge, which leads safely down to the saddle (999m) beneath Stob Coire nan Lochan. This is all obvious in good visibility. A long, easy ridge is followed NE up to the fine summit (1115m).

Two narrow ridges project from Stob Coire nan Lochan to enclose the north-facing upper Coire nan Lochan. Both make good descents; the northwest ridge is quicker but the northeast ridge has more scrambling interest. Going for the latter, head E from the summit and follow the narrow crest as it swings to the NE. From a broad shoulder at the base of the ridge (795m), drop W down easy slopes into the corrie. Head NW across the corrie floor to reach the head of a shallow gully (NN 152 553) located 50m N of the northernmost lochan. Bail easily down the gully into the head of the lower corrie.

Cross the head of the lower corrie and pick up a path on the true-right/east side of the stream. The path is a well-used approach route for teams climbing on Stob Coire nan Lochan and is likely to be well-tracked by late in the day. Follow the path easily down the corrie to a footbridge over the River Coe. A short incline then leads up to a large layby on the A82, some 3km east of the start point. It is easy to hitch from here. Alternatively, walk along the old military road, which runs down the glen a short distance beneath the south side of the A82.

The first junction of Summit Gully and a decision to bail; the main gully bed being chocker with unconsolidated snow - Paul James

29 Stob Coire Sgreamhach Sròn na Làirig

Crossing the final section of the Sròn na Làirig, with the Lairig Eilde stretching behind - Dave Smith

area
Glencoe,
West Highlands

start
NN 187 562

difficulty
Grade II

distance
11.1km

total ascent
955m

map
page 142

A belter of a ridge This lovely mountaineering route is perched high above the head of a long secluded glen. Its broad lower part offers a number of different starts over interesting mixed terrain. Higher up all variations converge to a narrow ridge, whose airiness is amplified by its grand position.

Doable in virtually all snow conditions, with the caveat that the north-facing finishing slopes, where the ridge abuts the main bulk of the mountain, require some care. The 4km-long approach walk is surprisingly quick and effortless. It is an outstanding ridge when climbed on its own but is even better when used to start a journey through the Bidean massif.

Stob Coire Sgreamhach Sròn na Làirig

Background The Lairig Eilde is the narrow glen that separates the Bidean nam Bian massif from Buachaille Etive Beag. It is open at both ends and a well-constructed path runs its entire length. Essentially it is a mountain pass (as the name Lairig suggests) that connects the head of Glencoe with Glen Etive. When compared to the nearby great corries of Bidean, the Lairig Eilde appears stark and almost featureless, but this is not to its detriment. It possesses a feeling of seclusion and tranquility, qualities hard to explain for a glen that is so easily accessed from a main road.

Stob Coire Sgreamhach (1072m) forms the southeast corner of the Bidean nam Bian massif. Seen from the Glencoe side it is an enticing mountain, with a pointed skyline and an imposing triangular north face that overlooks Coire Gabhail; the largest of Bidean's three great corries. When covered in snow the face has an alpine character. If blessed with névé it can be wandered up at will whilst staying within grade II. The traverse of the mountain's skyline however looks like it will be a full-on mission. This is an illusion; it is an uncomplicated ridge-walk that connects easily to Bidean's main summit.

The best winter mountaineering on Sgreamhach is found just outside the massif, tucked away at the head of the Lairig Eilde. Here a prominent subsidiary ridge projects into the open glen creating a compelling line. This is the Sròn na Làirig.

Description Start at a car park on the south side of the A82, at the head of Glencoe (NN 187 562), ½km east of where the road bends through a gorge. Head SW along a footpath signposted for Glen Etive, ignoring a minor left branch (which climbs southeast up to a col on Buachaille Etive Beag's summit ridge). Follow the main path over open ground before dropping to the Allt Lairig Eilde. Ford the steam and stroll up the glen on the now gently undulating path.

The prominent ridgeline of Sròn na Làirig can be seen directly ahead, coming straight out of the mountainside at the head of the glen. After 2.5km, a short distance before the path reaches its high point, break off right/W, aiming for the base of the ridge. In poor visibility head up the left /south side of a wide streambed, the Allt Coir' Eilde. After roughly 400m strike S uphill, following a vague burn that leads up to the first tier of outcrops directly beneath the ridge (NN 163 535).

The lower part of the ridge can be climbed at a number of places. A wide depression in the centre of the base is as good a start as any. The depression leads up to a flat-ish area, above which is a steep enclosed bay. Climb a series of ledges leading out from the left edge of the bay, or walk 70m or so to the right, around to a much easier leftward-leaning rocky couloir. Both options arrive at a broad girdle terrace beneath a steep nose.

Sròn na Làirig from the Lairig Eilde path

Stob Coire Sgreamhach Sròn na Làirig

Climb a mixed groove line starting from the left side of the terrace to gain the top of the nose. From now on Sròn na Làirig takes the form of a well-defined ridge in a lovely situation. With the way ahead no longer open to interpretation, climb up the left side of the ridge to the top of a tower. An exposed level section follows and leads to the head of a steep gully, which comes up from the right. Shimmy carefully across the narrow sneck forming the top of the gully and climb onto the main bulk of Stob Coire Sgreamhach.

The easy slopes above are not immune to avalanche. The steeper rocky ground out to the left is safer but much harder. Head up the most appropriate line to reach flat ground on Sgreamhach's southeast ridge. The mountain's perch-like summit lies 850m further up the ridge, over uncomplicated walking terrain.

Return The quickest and easiest descent is to go back down the Lairig Eilde. From the summit, head down the long SE ridge, to a wide col (741m) before a minor top. From here, bail NE down straightforward snow slopes into a shallow bowl. Continue descending in the same direction, in poor visibility sticking to the true-left bank of a burn (or shallow gorge) to avoid a band of small outcrops. On the floor of the glen trend right/E, to meet with the Lairig Eilde path at roughly its high point… and so to Glencoe.

Although spoilt for choice, one of the better options for continuing with a journey through the massif is to visit Bidean's main summit before descending via the unusual Coire Gabhail, the Lost Valley. An itinerary hard to match for the variety of terrain and scenery. From Stob Coire Sgreamhach, head down the defined W ridge to a narrow col, Bealach Dearg (944m). Now head NW up the narrow undulating ridge to the main summit of Bidean nam Bian (1150m).

Arriving at the top of Sròn na Làirig's main tower to be greeted by a timely snow squall - Dave Smith

Stob Coire Sgreamhach Sròn na Làirig

From Bidean's summit cairn, head NE, down steep broken ground to gain the top of a well-defined and level shoulder. Continuing north along the shoulder would culminate in a steep buttress, Diamond Buttress; so, from 50m before its end, drop easily right/NE onto a defined ridge, which leads safely down to the saddle (999m) beneath Stob Coire nan Lochan. This is all obvious in good visibility.

From the col, bail SE down an easy snow slope into an upper corrie. Exit the corrie to the NE and continue down convoluted slopes, staying north of a deep stream bed (almost a gorge). The upper part of the main valley has an impressive steep-sided gorge containing a high waterfall; this is well worth checking out. Head down the valley, following a rough path that undulates above the true-left bank of the stream.

The lower part of the valley is spookily flat and open, formed by a landslip that blocked the entrance; creating, over time, an alluvium build-up and the flat valley floor. The mouth of the valley is choked with a maze of huge boulders. Avoid the maze by following a path that climbs the hillside on the right/NE. The path traverses the hillside for a short distance, before dropping to the stream and crossing, via a boulder hop, to the true-left bank.

A scenic path now heads down towards Glencoe, staying a short distance above the steep wooded gorge. The River Coe is crossed by a footbridge, beyond which the path leads up to the A82, arriving at a small layby approximately 1.7km west of the start point (NN 173 567). Although a not a great distance to walk, the layby is a reliable hitching spot and on the correct side of the road.

The undulating ridge connecting Sgreamhach to Bidean's main summit and the third consecutive day of an inversion on the west coast - Steve Worth

30 Buachaille Etive Mòr Chasm to Crowberry

Entering the couloir that cuts through the upper cliffs of the Buachaille's southeast face - Ian Hey

area
Glencoe,
West Highlands

start
NN 233 531

difficulty
Grade II

distance
5.6km

total ascent
840m

map
page 151

An offbeat journey with an exploratory feel This wonderfully varied route follows a devious line through the maze of steep buttresses that cover the southeast flank of Stob Dearg. It is the only low-grade mountaineering line that crosses this otherwise complicated mountainside and is a thoroughly enjoyable day out.

A snowline of 450m ensures continuous snow from the entry ramps onwards. Easterly winds will give stable and, most likely, good conditions on this side of the mountain. Other wind directions certainly don't rule the route out but can give cause for care; the route crosses slopes with multiple aspects. There is no scope for abandoning this 950m-long traverse without venturing onto markedly more difficult ground; it needs to be either completed or reversed.

Buachaille Etive Mòr Chasm to Crowberry

Background Buachaille Etive Mòr sits in isolation at the junction between Glencoe and Glen Etive, on the edge of the flat expanse of Rannoch Moor. The mountain's 5.3km-long ridge contains five significant peaks, the highest and most easterly of which, Stob Dearg (1022m), is perhaps the most recognisable in Scotland; seen when approaching Glencoe from across Rannoch Moor, its steep north and east flanks taper to form a beautiful conical shaped mountain.

The northeast aspect of Stob Dearg is particularly impressive and is split by a series of towering buttresses and well-defined gullies, which provide a wealth of good winter climbing and mountaineering lines that are justifiably very popular. Moving around the mountain, towards Glen Etive, the eastern aspect brings into view an escalating stack of large walls, the highest of which sits beneath a prominent rock tower; Crowberry Tower. Further into Glen Etive, the southeast flank becomes increasingly chaotic, with its sprawl of irregular shaped buttresses presenting only a handful of natural lines. This part of the mountain is relatively neglected in winter.

The layout of the southeast flank is complicated to say the least. Its most distinctive feature is the deep fissure of the Chasm, cutting vertically into the left side of the face. With a little bit more scrutiny, a line of weakness reveals itself, running up diagonally rightwards through the maze of buttresses. This is the path of the Chasm to Crowberry Tower traverse, an enjoyable and offbeat way to climb Buachaille Etive Mòr.

Description Start at a small parking spot on the Glen Etive road (NN 233 531), 2.4km southwest of the junction with the A82. On a map, two streams can be seen converging near the road. The parking spot, a rough verge that can accommodate a handful of vehicles, sits between these two streams on the south side of the road. The northernmost stream drains from a deep and distinctive fissure on the flank of Stob Dearg. This is the Chasm.

The Chasm to Crowberry Tower traverse takes a rising rightward line across the mountainside and is easily picked out from the road. The traverse starts from where the Chasm narrows and steepens, then follows the only natural weakness through the maze of buttresses that sprawl up rightwards. The line becomes more obvious as it is approached. A prominent feature is a large overhanging rock at roughly the halfway mark.

Head up a vague track on the right/northeast side of the Chasm stream. Ascend to where the buttresses meet the gorge and it is no longer possible to walk up any higher (550m). Move right and climb either of two parallel ramps to gain the main fault line. Follow this natural line without difficulty, through ever-changing scenery, to where a steep sloping terrace passes beneath the overhanging rock. Beyond the rock the terrace opens into an enclosed steep-sided bay. Escape the bay by climbing a groove at its rear, which leads to the top of a small promontory.

The east face of Stob Dearg showing the snowline required for a decent Chasm to Crowberry traverse

Buachaille Etive Mòr Chasm to Crowberry

From the promontory, traverse right and descend a few metres into the top of a northeast-facing gully (which unnervingly drops steeply below). On the far side of the gully is the start of a couloir that breaches the upper cliffs of the southeast face. Sidle around the head of the gully to reach the couloir's narrow entrance and head up through the imposing cliffs. The couloir curves to the right through dramatic terrain, before narrowing to a snowy runnel. Climb the runnel to reach broken ground at the base of a large open snow slope.

On the upper right side of the slope, standing freely from the main bulk of the mountain, is a huge thumb of rock. This is Crowberry Tower. A short distance beneath the lowest rocks of the tower is the top of Curved Ridge, a much smaller fist of rock with a small cairn. Even if having experienced stable snow conditions on the entire traverse so far, crossing the open snow slope can still be suspect - it is angled perfectly for avalanche and reputedly collects snow from multiple directions. Gain the far side of the slope by an appropriate route and then head for the gully at the rear of Crowberry Tower.

Walk up the enclosed and easy-angled gully, which late in the day will likely have tracks from teams finishing Curved Ridge; a classic and very popular winter climb starting on the northeast side of the mountain. At the end of the gully, known as Crowberry Tower Gap, climb a leftward-leaning ramp on the left wall. At the top of the ramp, by a block, veer right and climb easily up to the summit slopes. A short walk then leads to Stob Dearg's isolated summit (1022m) and incredible, far-reaching views east, across Rannoch Moor.

Climbing the ramp from Crowberry Tower Gap - Ian Hey

Buachaille Etive Mòr Chasm to Crowberry

Return Leaving the summit of Stob Dearg can be confusing in poor visibility, where sloping, featureless terrain can contrive to pull you easily off course. Be really switched on. From the summit cairn, head SW along the blunt and fairly level summit ridge for 300m. Then head W, down easy ground (occasional small cairns) that leads to the flat col (874m) separating Coire na Tulaich to the north and Coire Cloiche Finne to the south. From the col, bail S down steep but uncomplicated slopes, aiming for the rib of high ground that runs down the centre of the corrie between the two burns. From the corrie's narrow mouth, head E across rough ground to meet with the Glen Etive road some 500m southwest of the start point.

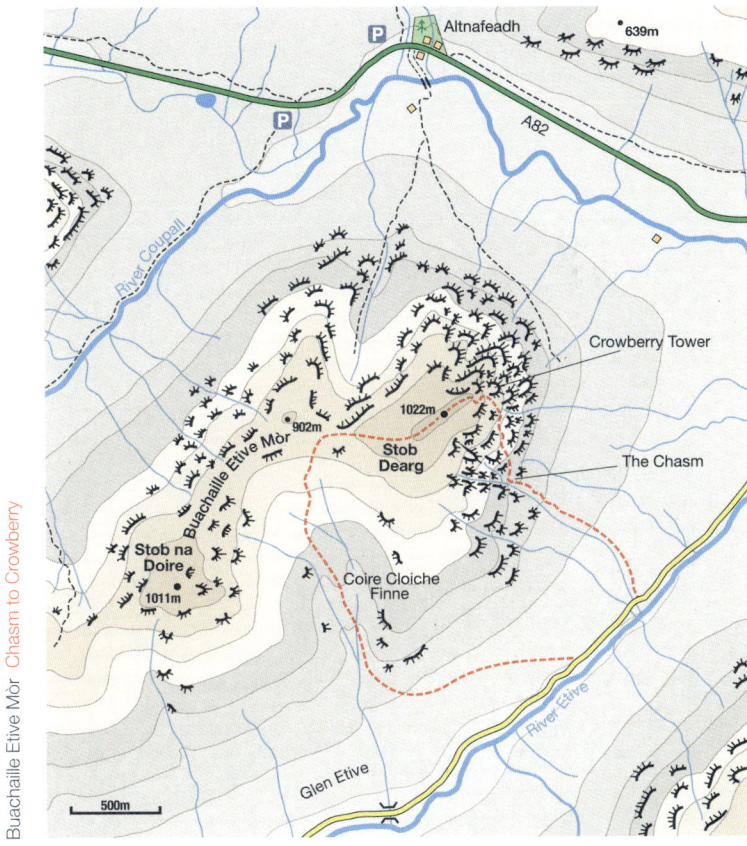

Notes

Mountain names The following list gives an English translation for the Gaelic name of each significant summit mentioned in the route descriptions. Gaelic hill names are beautifully descriptive; drawing not only on shape and colour but also what may have lived on the mountain, local folklore and even if the hill had a functional use. Given the many distinctions and regional nuances contained within the original names, the translations are the most likely modern interpretations. The Gaelic spelling corresponds to that found on the most recent Ordnance Survey map and may have changed or been anglicised with the passage of time. More on this subject, particularly the origin and tales behind the names can be found in Peter Drummond's fascinating book *Scottish Hill Names*.

01 Lochnagar (Lochan na Gaire) — little loch of the noisy sound
Beinn nan Chìochan (original name) — mountain of the breasts
Cac Càrn Beag — small cairn of poo

02 Cairn Gorm — blue cairn (but only appearing blue if seen from a great distance)
03 Am Monadh Ruadh (original name) — the red mountain-land (due to the pinkish hue of the local granite)
Stob Coire an t-Sneachda — point of the corrie of the snow
Fiachaill Coire an t-Sneachda — the toothed ridge of the corrie of the snow
Fiacaill a' Choire Chais — the toothed ridge of the steep corrie

04 An Teallach — the hearth or the forge
05 Sàil Liath — the grey heel (referring to a long, open slope at the end of a ridge)
Corrag Bhuidhe — the yellow forefinger or pointed one
Sgùrr Fiona — light coloured peak or possibly wine peak
Bidean a' Ghlas Thuill — mountain of the grey-green hollow

06 Beinn Eighe — file mountain
07 Sgùrr nan Fhir Duibhe — peak of the dark men (also frequently translated as 'the Black Carls')
Sgùrr Bàn — the white peak
Spidean Coire nan Clach — pointed peak of the stony corrie
Sail Mhòr — the big heel
Còinneach Mhòr — the big moss

08 Liathach — the grey-ish one
09 Stùc a' Choire Dhuibh Bhig — the steep conical hill of the little black corrie
Spidean a' Choire Lèith — pointed peak of the grey corrie
Mullach an Rathain — summit of the pulleys or summit of the row of pinnacles
Sgòrr a' Chadail — peak of the sleep

10 Beinn Alligin — possibly the jewelled or beautiful mountain
Sgùrr Mòr — big peak
Tom na Gruagaich — hill of the damsel

11 Beinn Damh — stag mountain
Spidean Coire an Laoigh — pointed peak of calf corrie
Sgùrr na Bana-Mhoráire — peak of the lady

12 Beinn Bhàn — the white mountain
A' Chìoch — the breast or the nipple

13 Sgorr Ruadh — the red peak
Beinn Liath Mhòr — the big grey mountain

14 Fuar Tholl — cold hole or cold hollow
Sgùrr a' Mhuilinn — peak of the mill

Mountain Names

15	Sgùrr nan Gillean	peak of the young men
	Am Bàsteir	possibly the cleft, also possible is the killer (but not the executioner)
	Sgùrr Beag	the little peak
16	Bruach na Frithe	slope of the wild mountainous land or deer forest
	Sgùrr a' Bhàsteir	uncertain, but as 'bàs' means death, possibly peak of the killer
	Sgùrr a' Fionn Choire	peak of the white corrie
17	Meallan Odhar	pale or greyish-brown mound or small hill
	Sgùrr na Forcan	peak of the little fork
	An Diollaid	the saddle (named due to the dip between the two summits)
18	Aonach air Chrith	the ridge of trembling
	Maol Chin-dearg	bald red hill
19	Beinn a' Chaorainn	mountain of the rowan
	Meall Bhàideanach	hill of the marsh or the drowned place
20	Creag Meagaidh	crag of the boggy place
	Sròn a' Choire	nose of the corrie (referring to a spur projecting from a hillside)
	Stob Poite Coire Ardair	peak of the pot of the high corrie
	Sròn Coire a' Chriochairein	nose of the boundary keeper's corrie
	Meall an t-Snaim	mound or hill at the junction
	Na Cnapanan	the little knobs
	Càrn Liath	grey cairn
21	Aonach Mòr	the big ridge
22	Càrn Beag Dearg	little red cairn
23	Càrn Dearg Meadhonach	middle red cairn
	Càrn Mòr Dearg	big red cairn
24	Ben Nevis	venomous or evil mountain (also possible, sky or heaven mountain)
	Càrn Dearg	red cairn
25	Stob Bàn	white peak
	Sgùrr an Iubair	peak of the yew
	Stob Choire a' Mhail	uncertain, 'Màl' means rent in modern Gaelic but this is tenuous
	Sgùrr a' Mhàim	peak of the large rounded hill or peak of the breast
26	Beinn a' Bheither	mountain of the thunderbolt or Celtic goddess of winter and death
	Sgorr Bhàn	the white peak
	Sgorr Dhearg	the red peak
	Sgorr Dhonuill	Donald's peak (though should really be Sgòrr Dhòmhnaill)
27	Aonach Eagach	the notched ridge
	Am Bodach	the old man
	Meall Dearg	red mound or hill
	Stob Coire Lèith	grey corrie peak
	Sgorr nam Fiannaidh	peak of the Fingalians - legendary Celtic warriors
28	Stob Coire nam Beith	peak of the corrie of the birches
29	Stob Coire Sgreamhach	peak of the loathsome corrie
	Stob Coire nan Lochan	peak of the corrie of the lochans
	Bidean nam Bian	peak of the mountains or chief of the hills, as the mountain's proper name is Bidean nam Beann (not 'bian', which means pelt)
30	Buachaille Etive Mòr	the big herdsman of Etive
	Stob Dearg	the red peak

Scotland's Winter Mountains with one axe

Calm and cold conditions, and an untracked ridge on a mid-January traverse of Liathach, Torridon - Kath James and Steve Worth

Descending the northeast ridge of Stob Coire nan Lochan on a journey through the Bidean nam Bian massif, Glencoe - Dom Fawcett

Deep inside South Castle Gully on Ben Nevis - Dave McGimpsey

Notes

Beinn a' Chaorainn East Ridge Since the first publication of this book there has been extensive felling of Badenoch Wood, the commercial plantation that sits between Beinn a' Chaorainn and the A86. New forestry tracks have been constructed, along with a metal bridge over the Allt na h-Uamha where previously there was only a fording point. These new tracks provide an alternative approach route to Beinn a' Chaorainn, which although longer is arguably easier-going, especially in very snowy conditions. The original route, along the side of the Allt na h-Uamha, is normally the quicker option and is by far the more aesthetic.

To approach using the forestry tracks, start at a junction with the A86 (NN 390 818), 1km west of the Allt na h-Uamha stone bridge. There is parking for about 5 vehicles, plus a layby 600m further west. Head up the forestry track, which after two sharp bends leads ENE up the hillside. After 1km, at the first junction, turn left and follow the track NW for 400m to another junction. Turn right and follow the track NE for 500m to intersect with the original route on the edge of the plantation.

The map for Beinn a' Chaorainn has been updated and now shows both approaches to the mountain. However, it doesn't differentiate between felled and non-felled areas of the wood; the felling is ongoing. And anyway, on the ground, by its resemblance to a battlefield, any area of felled plantation will be easy to identify for years.